YO-ABI-452

88

EUROPEAN and ORIENTAL RUGS

EUROPEAN and ORIENTAL RUGS

for pleasure and investment

JACK FRANSES

ARCO PUBLISHING COMPANY, INC
New York

Published by
ARCO Publishing Company, Inc.
219 Park Avenue South,
New York, N.Y. 10003

Printed in Great Britain

Acknowledgements

My Late Father
My sister Sandra
*S. Franses (Carpets) Ltd.
*The Hermitage Museum, Leningrad
*The Victoria and Albert Museum, London
*C. John
*Eastern Carpets Ltd.
*Anglo Afghan Carpet Company
Rumanian Embassy
Finish Embassy
Norwegian Embassy
Indian Embassy
Pakistan Embassy
*Perez Ltd.
*R. Franses & Son
*Sotheby & Company
*V. Franses, Esq.

The author acknowledges the help and photographs which were supplied by the above.*

Preface

My sole aim in writing this book is to assist you in what might, at first, seem an impossible task, that is to teach you the way to identify carpets and rugs. Although each carpet weaving centre deserves at least a chapter, and in some cases many, I have condensed the most relevant points in the best order, by use of a master key. Using a key will, of course, quickly build up your confidence—without the confidence we are unable to buy for pleasure or investment; for carpets can be said to be one of the most underrated of the arts, due mostly to lack of literature and knowledge.

CONTENTS

List of Colour Plates

List of Black & White Illustrations

List of Black & White Photographs

Introduction

The origin of carpet weaving is very remote. In the tomb of Mehenwetre who was Chancellor and Steward to the Royal Palace of Pharaoh Mentuhotep during his reign (2000 B.C.), complete wooden model representations of the daily life of the estate of this noble Egyptian were found. Perhaps the most charming discovery in this collection was that showing a group of women spinning flax with quaint old distaffs and spindles. Some of these threads were actually found intact after 4,000 years!

At the moment an experiment is in progress in Egypt where a Nile boat, made of papyrus reed, is being built with the idea of sailing it to South America. If it completes this arduous journey it may suggest an answer to the speculation concerning the Peru civilisation and the pyramids in Mexico. It could prove that America might well have been discovered between 2,500 and 4,000 years ago! I wish Thor Heyerdahl—GOOD LUCK.

I believe that carpet collecting is almost inborn. The first contact one has with carpets of any sort is when we are infants crawling around on our hands and knees and digging our little fingers into the pile. Our next encounter is when we are old enough to play hopscotch on the designs, or cards, marbles or ha'pennies using the carpet as a large games board. I have often wondered whether any collectors recall, in their child-hood days, the first contact that they had.

Many people who have been in the Middle East in military, diplomatic or other services and now have time to spare, find themselves sitting very comfortably in an Oriental carpet store, drinking black coffee and listening to the fascinating stories which can be told. One can spend many days bargaining and seeing the different types of rugs to be bought. The range is so great that it is very hard for the layman to absorb— but *what a challenge!*

Where do we start to learn when there are seldom signatures to trace the maker, and when each country and each town copies the other's designs. They all look the same—OR DO THEY?

1. Seventeenth century Indian; 15 ft. × 9 ft. 10 in. Sold at Sotheby's, £4,800 (1969).

Oriental carpets as an investment

It is surprising how few people consider Oriental carpets as an investment. Antiques, *objets d'art*, paintings and furniture over 100 years old or thereabouts, yes, but carpets and rugs that you walk on and may wear out, do not add up to a sound investment for the average person. With those who are enlightened it is a far different proposition. Let us consider some facts. There is the wearability of an Oriental carpet compared with the average Wilton or Axminster carpet sold today. The A1 Axminster has forty-nine tufts per square inch and the average Wilton approximately sixty: neither has a base knot. Their wool is blended (the method used to mix the cheaper and better grades of wool before spinning) and mill spun, which has the tendency of shedding the loose ends for many months before the pile settles down. The life expectancy is from ten to fifteen years, and the colours are sharp aniline dyes which tend to fade, the designs are set in complete balance repeating every two or three feet. Their secondhand value after purchase decreases by 50 per cent which then depreciates gradually until eventually no value remains. Of course, they have their uses, as have the clothes we wear, to be discarded when desired or necessary.

How different this is to the Oriental carpet. The Oriental carpet has from 150 to as many as 1,200 knots per square inch. The pile is long or short, it is lustrous and has a firmly based knot (either Persian or Ghiordes). Its wool is hand-spun on all the early carpets and semi-antiques and this does not shed loose ends so rapidly. The life expectancy of the base knot is from 50 to 150 years and more, for we find many examples of sixteenth- and seventeenth-century Oriental rugs in perfect condition, save for minor repairs. The wools are treated gently, unlike the treatment in modern factories today, where harsh

3

scouring is employed to remove grease and dirt. The dyes are mainly vegetable, such as madder (red), reseda (yellow), saffron (yellow), indigo (blue), cochineal (carmine red which is made from the body of the female insect), pomegranate skins (orange), nutshells, oak-bark, or iron ore (browns) and many more plants, roots, etc. which help to make up the beautiful blends of natural colours. These are enhanced during age, because unlike aniline dyes they do not fade but mellow, increasing their beauty. The designs are hereditary and some have been passed down from as early as 500 years B.C. This is indeed substantiated by the discovery of a well preserved rug, in 1947, by a Russian archaeologist in a grave mound of a Prince of Alti; it has been established that he reigned in the fifth century B.C. The Alti rug, made of wool, was preserved by an unusual combination of circumstances (see Russia gen. text).

In paintings from the fourteenth century one can see very fine examples of Oriental rugs, which were used as backgrounds by the finest painters. The designs were drawn by unknown artists dating back to the earliest beginnings. Each design has its own particular flow and gentle tranquillity which is enhanced by its individuality.

The designs are primitive and homely. There are changes in the ground colour and in other colours in the rug. These changes are due either to the wool being dyed at different periods or to the wool being laid out in the sun to dry. Thereby one gets variations of each colour which makes for gentleness and beauty.

The value of Oriental rugs, contrary to machine-made goods, increases substantially throughout their life providing they are kept in good condition. They should not be allowed to deteriorate through lack of periodical expert cleaning and minor repairs which are needed on the sides and ends. The best investments are rugs in perfect condition and of fine quality made prior to the 1900s. Most of these come from Persia (Iran), Turkey or India. For example, a fine quality Persian Kashan rug, woven in the 1900s, bought in the late 1950s between £90 and £140 would, in good condition today (1970) fetch between £500 and £600. One can see by this example that not only has one had the advantage of possessing a beautiful rug for a number of years, but at the same time a sound investment has been made, often unknowingly. Most people are surprised to learn that their rugs are of such value. The cheaper quality rugs which in the same period cost £25 to £40 have only increased to a maximum of £120 today. Unfortunately, in the case of Turkestan rugs (Bokharas) the market has been swamped by imitations from Pakistan and the increase in value has again been of lesser extent. For example, a rug costing £45 in the 1950s would today (1970) be worth about £150. However, in all cases the money has been invested wisely for one has to consider the fact that other flooring would have been worn out and replaced at an ever increasing cost.

An investment in Oriental rugs is sound. The main problem which arises is the lack of knowledge. Books are sometimes misleading as they tend to generalise and people who read them and study them word for word usually find themselves in a muddle.

When choosing a Persian rug the most important thing is that the rug should be pleasing to the eye of the purchaser. One has to live with these rugs for a lifetime and no matter how finely made, or how long the history, they must possess an attractive appearance. Exceptions can be made by the collector, who wants examples of each type of rug, irrespective of colour or furnishing. The best advice one can give is to find a reputable dealer, who specialises in Oriental rugs. Put yourself in his hands and ask the following important questions:

THE TEN RULES FOR BUYING

1. Is the rug of vegetable dye?
2. Is the rug of aniline dye?
   (Aniline dyes were introduced in approximately 1870, vegetable dyes were used up to 1930, although 1914 was the turning point. There are, of course, rugs made with vegetable dyes today, but they are few and far between. Therefore, rugs which have age and are of vegetable dye are invariably antique, i.e. over 100 years old.)
3. Is the rug in good condition?
   (A ninety-year-old rug, worn out, is of very little use, as there are quite a few examples of seventeenth-century and eighteenth-century rugs available at reasonable prices.)
4. Has the rug been repaired, if so, would you please show me the repairs?
   (One must always expect to find a certain amount of repair work in most rugs, this does not detract much from the value. Unless the repairs have been executed badly.)

5. Is the rug complete, i.e. are there any borders, ends or sides missing?
   (This can reduce the value of the rug quite considerably.)
6. Would you repurchase this rug from me in four years, and perhaps show me a profit?
7. Have you given a full and true description and why is this a sound investment?
8. Has this been process washed?
   (This is a treatment given to modern rugs to make them look old.)
9. Has this been chemically bleached, removing all colours save two or three?
   (For example, Golden Afghans.)
10. Has the rug a natural patina?
    (The early rugs were made of wool taken from the breast of the sheep; being the most protected part of the sheep the wool has its own natural lustre.)

Above all get to know your dealer well, treat him more as a friend than just another shopkeeper. You will find that he is more than willing to explain the idiosyncracies of the weavers' art, and you will spend many pleasant and rewarding hours. You will learn that when a good rug is in your possession it becomes part of you, one of the family, and it will radiate the love and devotion that has been put into its creation.

Coupled with all these facts is the cost of weaving hand-knotted rugs today, for it takes as long as nine months to weave a fine quality rug. Basing this on present day wages of a master weaver (say about £3,000 per annum), it seems impossible that one can still buy a hand-made rug of this quality for between £350 and £400. The value is tremendous, and the investment speaks for itself.

Rug weaving centres of the world

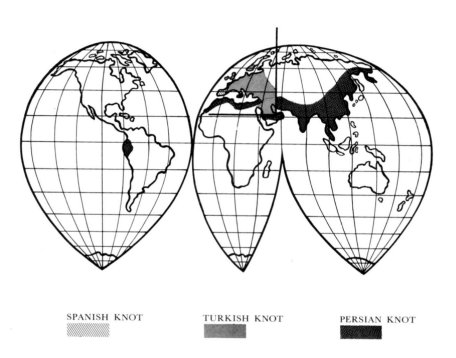

SPANISH KNOT

TURKISH KNOT

PERSIAN KNOT

RUG WEAVING AND CENTRES

The first key of rug identification is—WHERE does the rug come from?

Plate 1: Map of the world—red shows areas; dots shown in black are the centres, one dating back to 500 years B.C.

The seven keys to identification

1. Design [*See appendix for diagrams*]

When you look at the Alti carpet (woven 500 years B.C.), you see the first example of a well-balanced design, with the simple, primitive uniqueness that one finds in pottery and which is far in advance of the cave dwellers' wall scratchings.

1. The Alti rug (500 B.C.); 6 ft. 6 in. × 6 ft., *see Russian text–gen.* Page 131.

Through the ages, in the Middle and Far East, each centre kept to its own designs, proud of its traditions; but, of course, due to marriages, the camel trains, wars and the change of power, fine weavers and artists were moved to new capitals. Yet up to the eighteenth century, through all this turmoil, the designs seem to have survived.

During the thirteenth century, a centre for carpet weaving was set up in Spain. The designs were bold, floral and with a slight Turkish influence. The Spaniards led the way into Europe and soon the other countries followed suit: England with its Turkey work, France with the famous Savonnerie carpets, Russia (Georgia), the Ukranians, Austria, Poland and the Scandinavian countries with their own styles.

The majority of designs in Europe were floral and were influenced by the fashionable Chinese material designs, which followed the austere Gothic and ornate Renaissance periods. The designs were of a light gay nature with ribbons, garlands of flowers, fruit and cameos.

A CLOSER LOOK AT DESIGNS

Designs copied by other countries show a distinct variation from the original, for example, Turkish weavers were asked to copy Chinese designs—the result was that some of the floral motifs looked Chinese but the majority looked Turkish (foreign). The wool used was heavier, the dyes and knots different and, therefore, even to the layman identification is simple.

The same rule applies to each country. Although today copying is prevalent, the copiers give themselves away. Sometimes by over-elaborating a simple tribal rug or by colours that were never originally used. Take for example, the Bokhara rug (from Turkestan). These rugs have been copied in Persia and Pakistan, and a green or pale blue ground is used, and these colours were never used in Tukestan. If you compare a Pakistan Bokhara with a genuine Turkestan rug, you will soon notice the over-elaboration.

Let us divide the world up and see the different types of designs each country has.

1. *Persia*

(*a*) Majority of designs are fine, ornate florals.
  i. Typical Persians, are the Kashans.

2. *Turkey*

(*a*) Strong bold designed. Modern. Turkish carpet.
(*b*) Similar to Persian are the Hereke's.
(*c*) French design Savonnerie—(made in the 1920s).
(*d*) Normal anatolian.

3. *Kazakestan*

(*a*) Bold geometrical design Kazak.

4. *Caucasus*

(*a*) Geometrical designs.
(*b*) Bold floral Karabagh.

5. *India*

(*a*) Indo Ispahan.
(*b*) Typical Indian. Proper.
(*c*) Typical spray corners design. Modern. Chinese design.
(*d*) French Aubusson designs.

6. *Turkestan*

(*a*) Elephants' foot design.

7. *Eastern Turkestan*

(*a*) Samarkand design.

8. *Pakistan*

(*a*) Copiers of most designs.

9. *Afghanistan*

(*a*) Large elephants' foot design. Afghan (compare with Bokhara's).

10. *China*

(*a*) Antique Chinese.
(*b*) 1900–1930 period Chinese.
(*c*) Modern Chinese.

11. *Russia*

(*a*) Ukranian.
(*b*) Kelim—a reversable fine, hand-woven, tapestry rug.

12. *Rumania*

(*a*) Floral kelims. From: the beginning to 1950.
(*b*) Geometrical kelims.
(*c*) Modern copies, Persian designs—twentieth century.

13. *Czechoslovakia*

(*a*) Modern (savonnerie design carpets), floral (like French).

14. *Poland*
(*a*) Persian polonaise.
(*b*) Polish polonaise.

15. *Scandinavia*
(*a*) Primitive designs and floral.

16. *Spain*
(*a*) Old quenca.
(*b*) New, modern savonneries as French.

17. *France*
(*a*) Old and new alike.

18. *England*
(*a*) Adam carpets.

19. *Ethiopia*
(*a*) Like modern Samarkand designs, first made 1956.

20. *Egypt*
(*a*) Old carpets, three main periods.

21. *Greece*
(*a*) Turkish type carpets, Greek spartas.

The twenty-one countries are not the only ones, which have organised carpet weaving. My aim is to give you a general picture of designs. Now let us try to narrow the field by joining countries by means of design-relationship.

1. FLORAL/FRENCH/ADAM—Savonneries designs
   England, France, Russia, Rumanian Kelims, Czechoslovakia, India, Chinese, Caucasian (Karabagh), Spain.

2. ELEPHANTS' FOOT—Bokhara designs made in Persia, Turkestan, Afghanistan, Pakistan, Belouchistan.

3. GEOMETRICAL
   Kazakestan, Caucasian, Turkish–Armenia, Shiraz in Persia, Pakistan copies, Ardebil in Persia.

4. CHINESE DESIGNS
   China, India, Chinese spartas from Greece and Turkey.

5. PERSIAN DESIGNS
   Persia, India, Turkey, Persian polonaise, Modern European copies.

6. TURKISH
Turkey, Greece, Pakistan copies.

7. SCANDINAVIAN
Scandinavia.

8. EASTERN TURKESTAN—Samarkand designs
Kashgar, Kansu, Ethiopia, China, Mongul, Khotan, Yarkand.

From twenty-one countries to eight main types of designs. Each with its own distinctive flow. The purer the design the greater the difference. By studying the eight groups of plates, you will be able to see that you can tell, without help, each rug's origin.

THINGS TO LOOK FOR IN DESIGNS WHICH ARE ALIKE

(a) Savonnerie designs—Notice the difference between Chinese motifs, European and Indian. You should be able to see whether the design is Chinese, European or Indian.

(b) Persian and Turkish designs—Notice the difference between the motifs, once again test yourself by looking at the plates, or any carpet book from the library, covering the names.

(c) Elephants' foot designs—At this stage it is better to be satisfied to distinguish this design from others. We will, however, go into detail in later sections on Turkestans and Afghanistans.

(d) Geometrical—By looking at the plates, you should be able to see the difference between the Shiraz (Persian) and the Caucasian. Notice the hooks to the shiraz medallion, also see other differences as shown under the heading Shiraz (Persia) and the Caucasian section. Kazakestan rugs are that much bolder.

(e) Scandinavian—Shows its complete individuality in rugs, but an attachment to the Ukraine in their kelims.

(f) Samarkands—Typical Samarkand: i. Ethiopian copy of a Samarkand; ii. Mongul—A cross between a Samarkand and Chinese.

(g) Egypt—Once you have seen a Cairo carpet, you will not forget it easily.

Key no. 1
We have now covered all the different designs generally used

12

—we shall now try to narrow the field once again and try to make only *three types*.

By dividing the world in three, in this way, you should be able to tell from which part a rug comes. Once this is established, we can look again and try to get closer to its home—a process of elimination.

EASTERN DESIGNS

1. *The Far East*—India, Eastern Turkestan, (Samarkands) and China.

PERSIAN DESIGNS

2. *Middle East*—Greece, Turkey, Persia, Caucasus, Egypt, Afghanistan, Turkestan (Bokhara).

FLORAL DESIGNS

3. *Europe*—(Savonnerie).

Now try a test, try to put all rugs into one of the above three catagories. Then see if you can try to find their country of origin. Test yourself with the plates.

First we look and next we inspect—remember to avoid making a decision until you have checked all points, which can, and will no doubt, alter your opinion. It is important not to say anything until you are backed with facts, otherwise you will be sorry for speaking too soon.

We should not forget that the designs and combination of colours are the most fascinating and alluring things they have to offer; quality does not enter into it until you have handled the rug, it only acts as a better foundation to a beautiful article, of course, it will last longer if required for hard wear.

Designs have been passed down from generation to generation since the earliest beginning. They have great meaning, if not religious, superstitious.

SIGNS & MOTIFS

TARANTULAS SCORPION

CROWS FOOT RAIN DOOR COMB OF CLEANLINESS HAND WITH EYE

1 · 1A · 1B. TREE OF LIFE
2. CYPRESS TREE
3. POMEGRANATES
4. CAMELS

5. DOGS
6 · 6A. PEACOCKS
7. DOVE
8. ROOSTER

14

Tree of life	Symbol of eternal life.
Cypress trees	Survival in after life.
Pomegranates	Riches in abundance.
Camels	Wealth and happiness.
Dogs	Drive away all undesirables including witches, robbers and diseases.
The Peacock	A sacred bird.
The Dove	Peace and good omens.
Rooster	A herald of glory and victory.
	A crow's foot.
	Door.
	Rain.
	Comb of cleanliness.
	The Hand with an Eye—as it is said that a father should watch over his son until he is one score and six years.
Scorpions and Tarantulas	These are put into rug designs, so that children get used to seeing them; for it is only when one panics that one is likely to be bitten.

Remember also that the terrain plays a great part in designs, for example Caucasian rugs are woven in a mountainous region and the rugs are geometrical. As you travel southwards you find that as the terrain alters, so do the designs. A significant point being, that you can only design what you have seen or what you have been taught, handed down from the previous generation.

Everytime you look at a rug, just see if it is symmetrical; to your surprise you will find that, although at first glance it is, on closer scrutiny—the medallion is six inches out of alignment, side motifs differ, etc., but what simplicity and charm, no boring, repetitive designs to dull your life.

2. Knot

The first thing I want you to do is to look at the world map, at a glance you will be able to see the *Dividing Line* between East and West. In the area west of the line, which has been shaded, the Turkish (Ghiordes) knot is used, but east of the line, shown dotted, Sehna (Persian) knot is used. While in Spain the Spanish knot is used.

By knowing the knot you are now able to use your second key to identify your rug.

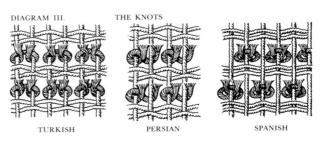

DIAGRAM III.   THE KNOTS

TURKISH   PERSIAN   SPANISH

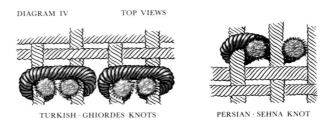

DIAGRAM IV   TOP VIEWS

TURKISH · GHIORDES KNOTS   PERSIAN · SEHNA KNOT

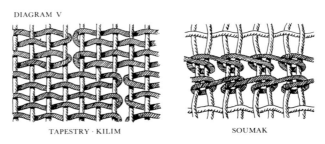

DIAGRAM V

TAPESTRY · KILIM   SOUMAK

Study the knot diagrams carefully and if you are able to see examples of rugs with all the knots shown you will soon be able to tell the difference. If you find difficulty in differentiating between them ask your local dealer to show you. The most important thing to remember is shown on 'top views of knots, which are:

(*a*) The Turkish knot has a band of wool, and its two woollen ends sticking out.

(*b*) The Persian knot does not at first appear to have a knot until you look sideways on and see the wool wrapped around the warp.

And, finally, the Spanish knot: note that the knot is tied to alternate warp threads and easy identification is possible.

Let us now summarize and put *Key No. 2* into action.

Key No. 2

1. If it has a Turkish knot is it made west of the *Dividing Line* but including the Caucasus, Tabriz (Persia) and a few Kurdish tribes.
2. If it has a (Sehna) Persian knot it is made east of the line.
3. If it has a Spanish knot it is made in Spain.

Therefore, if you look at a rug and you are not certain whether it is Persian or Turkish, you have only to look at its knot and you can now be more definite. There are only a few towns in Persia which use the Turkish knot, and if you study their types, designs and dyes, applying the other keys, your identification will be correct.

3. Dyes

Unfortunately, about half a century ago huge quantities of rugs and carpets were woven in Persia for the European markets; weavers were asked to make use of the discovery of synthetic dyes, for quickness and cheapness, and these were freely used. Certain colours especially, such as orange, red, green and light blue, were much too glaring to suit those of refined taste and resort to chemical treatment was made in order to subdue them, and produce the patina effect. The acid used in the chemical treatment of the colours tended to rot the basic strands of the rugs, and many thousands have been ruined from this cause during the past forty-five years. Naturally, great improvements have been made in the methods of handling the synthetic dyes, and today complete rotting of the strands seldom takes place, but even now this process tends to slightly weaken the materials, and rugs which have been chemically treated are not recommended.

17

VEGETABLE DYES

Vegetable dyes, such as madder (red); reseda (yellow); saffron (yellow); indigo (blue); cochineal (carmine red, which is made from the body of the female insect); pomegranate skins (orange); nutshells, oak-bark or iron ore (browns) and many more plants, roots, etc. help to make up the beautiful blends of natural colours. These are enhanced during age because unlike aniline dyes they do not fade but mellow, increasing their beauty.

HOW TO DETECT THE DIFFERENCE BETWEEN VEGETABLE AND ANILINE DYES

Let us first look at the process of vegetable dyeing to find a number of points to base our judgment on.

(a) There will be variations of shade in each colour. For example, on a plain red ground rug with a medallion centre, the red will have different bands of red (this is known as an 'abrush'). This is due to the wool being dyed at different periods.

(b) If you were dyeing madder red, you would steep the wool in a vat for say twelve hours with madder roots. After that time on the boil, you would then spread the wool out on the ground in the sun to dry. The wool, which is on the top, would dry quickly and the wool underneath, which has a heavy residue of dye left in it is darker. Between the top and the bottom layer, there might be as many as ten shades, which when drawn out for spinning will be either bands of colours or each strand or knot will contain the ten shades. With this variation, the lighter shades catch the light and reflect the colour in a most delightful way, giving perhaps a false patina.

What to look for in vegetable dyes

(a) Look for bands of colour (be careful, false bands are put in by modern weavers to give this effect).

(b) In order to double check, look at each strand of wool and make certain that it varies.

(c) Most wools used, with the exception of a few cases, were hand spun and are not two, three or four ply yarns.

(d) No loss of colour, except in aubergine and mauve.

(e) Bright colours.

18

3. A section of a Turkey carpet.

What to look for in aniline dyes
(a) Fading—loss of colour (maybe at one end or one side *or* on the tips of the wool).
(b) Plain flat colours.
(c) Change of colours, plum reds to grey, or blue to slate grey.
(d) Most wool used is mill spun—two, three and four ply yarns.

In summing up, I would like to say that I hope I have not painted too black a picture as far as aniline dyes are concerned, because there are some wonderful rugs to be found containing them, and also the chrome dyes (another synthetic).

There is no substitute for experience, so take every opportunity to look at the wools and dyes of rugs at your local museum, and your eye will soon detect the difference (a good idea is to wear a colourful aniline sweater or cardigan and make the comparisons).

THE SIGNIFICANCE OF COLOURS

Green, being a holy colour, was forbidden for use in ground colours (unless Prayer Rugs), until the 1930s, when commercial weaving under foreign pressure for export, demanded its introduction.

Each colour has its own meaning:
Black—Revolt, destruction.
Brown—Good harvest, fertility.
White—Purity and peace and colour of mourning.
Red—Happiness and joy.
Green—Spring and re-birth.
Sky-blue—National colour of Persia, and colour of mourning.
Indigo—Solitude.
Purple or *violet*—The king's colours.
Gold—Wealth and power.

It is not difficult to see how each colour derived its meaning, for example:
Green—spring, re-birth and paradise, spring is easy to understand—and re-birth as well, as the flowers are re-born amidst the greenery, paradise must certainly be green.
Brown—*earth* must mean fertility.

And so on, each having its own simple meaning, simple and primitive maybe, but are not we all in many ways.

Perhaps, that is why we are so attracted to the Oriental rugs, and also why they seem to grow on us; it is a pity that some are

19

4. Chinese. *Circa* 1950.

so blind to such beauty, which is virtually at their fingertips.

DYES

Key No. 3

When your eye is better trained you will be able to look at rug dyes and be able to place them in an area, for example:

1. Sand yellows, deep indigo, aubergine, plum, mauve reds, and blue-greens, the green being different from any other used and the most obvious.

    (*a*) Far-eastern dyes from China to the eastern part of Persia and the Meshed and Khorrasan districts.

2. Madder reds, brick reds, terracotta and pistachio greens.

    (*a*) Western central Persia up to the Caucasus.

3. The pinks tend towards mauve, slate blues, bright reds and olive greens.

    (*a*) Turkey. THREE different looks, another key for identification.

(Please note: that as the European carpet designs are so different, I have not included them.)

4. Wool

The Persian country being ideal for the rearing of sheep, goats and camels, supplied abundant quantities of the best wool for textile purposes, while the inhabitants' knowledge of vegetable dyes, their inborn sense of design, colour and their weaving art, contributed to maintain the unquestioned supremacy of their product all over the world. The rugs appreciated by each of the three classes of Persian society differed decisively. Those made for the kings and princes were magnificent works of art, in most instances designed by the foremost painters of the day and constructed with the very finest materials obtainable. The petty princes local chieftains and rich merchants had rugs which, though less rich and artistically important, were nevertheless of admirable beauty. The nomads and villagers aimed more at utility and made handsome but unpretentious rugs of simple patterns and few colours.

Purity of materials is all-important to the quality of a carpet. For some of the very finest Persian carpets even the sheep were sometimes bred and tended like children, in order to prevent their wool from matting! Even today, in two carpets made to the same pattern with the same dyes by the same weavers, and differing only in grade of wool, one may by worth three times the other!

PATINA

The friction of the foot gives carpets a natural silk sheen (patina) reflecting the beautiful vegetable dyes, and lending a tone of richness that no modern carpet can equal. Moreover, if proper care is taken, these rugs will last almost for ever. They have beauty and utility and will give to their owners a thrill of pleasure and of satisfaction which will endure while the rug endures and this will be far longer than an ordinary lifetime.

Wool texture

The areas where sheep are reared have an obvious effect on the texture of the wools. Once again, as with dyes, we will make the divisions.

Areas

1. China and Eastern Turkestan.
2. India.
3. Turkestan.
4. Pakistan.
5. Persia and the Caucasus.
6. Turkey.
7. Europe.

What to look for (Key No. 4)

1. *China and Eastern Turkestan*—Long, uneven cut wool, almost shaggy, on older carpets. (New Chinese look like silk, this is because the wool is given a chemical lustre.)
2. *India*—Dry almost cotton look, but tough.
3. *Turkestan*—Short tough pile, silky look.
4. *Pakistan*—Medium pile, very soft wool, which you can depress and has little or no resilience. Silky look is due to chemical washing, which does not last.
5. *Persia and the Caucasus*—Short tough pile with resilience (please note, in eastern parts of Persia and Kazakestan the pile tends to be a little longer).

21

6. *Turkey*—Long, heavy, lustrous pile on most modern rugs, old pieces tend to have the Persian look.
7. *Europe*—Long, heavy pile, tough but with a sheen.

5. Side cords

From the diagram (see appendix) you can see the main differences in the side cords used by weavers. This is only extended by: Firstly, Kazaks sometimes use bands of colours, but still maintain a treble cord (see diagram D). Secondly, old Chinese use a white cotton, single or double cord. Thirdly, two towns in Persia use mauve silk cords on their woollen rugs (see diagram A).

Key No. 5

1. Most carpets have their single side cords overcast in wool, silk or cotton, (see A).
2. The rugs which are different are as follows:
   Shiraz (B), Meshed Belouche (C), Turkish, Belouchistan, Tabriz, Caucasian, Kazaks (D).
3. Silk cords are used on old Kashans and Sehna rugs.

It, therefore, follows that if you find rugs in categories B, C, and D, they are soon identified. For example, it is hard for a beginner to tell the difference between a Shiraz and a Shirvan (Caucasian), (both geometrical designs). An easy way is by using key no. 5, the cords (diagram B), and key no. 2, the knot. The knot should be Persian for a Shiraz. Ghirdes for a Caucasian.

   i. Shiraz has a Persian knot and bands of different coloured wools overcast.

   ii. Shirvan has Turkish knot and double plain cord.

6. Ends (warp) fringes

Warps run the length of the rug through to the fringes
Points to note:
1. What are warps made of?
2. What colours to look for (if natural or dyed).

Point No. 1

Warps are made of: silk, cotton, wool, hair (goat and camel), goats' fleecy undercoat mixed with wool or hair, hemp and flax.

Point No. 2

Warps are sometimes dyed and their colour depends on their make-up. For example, silk rugs either natural or dyed gold, although six coloured warps extending into a warp fringe, with an interlaced weft sometimes occur.

Other points to note are the make-up. For example: cotton is white, hemp is brown (dry), camel and goats' hair mixed with wool is fawn to soft brown and flax is brown (dry).

Key No. 6

Warps used by different countries.

(a) *China*—Cotton.
(b) *Asia Minor*—Silk or wool on old rugs, although since 1948 cotton has been used extensively.
(c) *Spain*—Wool, goat, linen, later cotton.
(d) *France*—Wool, later carpets flax.
(e) *England*—Hemp or flax, wool (eighteenth century), cotton (end of nineteenth century).
(f) *India*—Cotton, hemp or silk.
(g) *Caucasus*—Wool (modern Erivan rugs have cotton).
(h) *Turkestan*—Wool, hair and wool, never cotton.
(i) *Pakistan*—Cotton.
(j) *Persia*—Cotton, silk or wool.
    1. Kelim carpets made in India have cotton warps.
    2. Kelim carpets made in Russia and Persia have wool warps.

How you will use *Key No. 6*, for example:
(h) A Bokhara rug in Turkestan will have wool and hair warp (fringes).
(i) A Bokhara design rug made in Pakistan will have a cotton warp (fringes).

7. Weft (Kelim ends)

(Kelim ends)—the weft runs the width of the rug

Points to note:
1. What are wefts made of?
2. Colour of weft (if dyed or natural products).
3. How many weft strands are used in between each row of knots.
4. When crossed with the warp ends (fringes) they are called 'Kelim ends', and can be made into very pleasing designs. These are usually found in marriage or presentation rugs and tend to increase their value.

Key No. 7

Wefts used by different countries.

(*a*) *China*—Cotton, all cotton Kelim ends.

(*b*) *Asia Minor*—Silk, wool, post 1908 mostly cotton. Bergama rugs have made a feature of small diamond designs or people on their Kelims, and bands of madder red throughout weft.

(*c*) *Spain*—Wool, goat, linen—no feature of Kelim ends.

(*d*) *France*—Wool, flax—no feature of Kelim ends.

(*e*) *England*—Flax, hemp, later wool and cotton—no feature of Kelim ends.

(*f*) *Indian*—Cotton, *dyed blue* on Amritza and Peristan—no feature of Kelim ends.

(*g*) *The Caucasus*—Wool, Derbents have blue soumac stitch *Kelim ends*.

(*h*) *Turkestan*—Wool, hair (never cotton), old Bokharas used to have Kelim ends up to one metre at each end, in madder red with very fine indigo lines or triangular designs.

(*i*) *Pakistan*—Cotton—no feature of Kelim ends.

(*j*) *Persia*—Cotton, wool or silk, *dyed red* on Shiraz (also making a feature of its Kelim ends), *dyed blue* on Kashan, Mahal and Kirman.

(*k*) *Kazakestan*—Wool, goat hair and mixture usually having two or three heavy weft strands—no feature of Kelim ends.

(*l*) *Samarkand*—Cotton—no feature of Kelim ends.

(*m*) *Moroccan*—Cotton or wool, they have sometimes as many as six weft strands in between each row of knots—no feature of Kelim ends.

(*n*) *Belouchistan*—Cotton in modern rugs, old rugs prior to 1925 have wool, goat hair and camel hair. They make a special feature of their Kelim ends and very many unusual designs are seen.

(*o*) *Afghanistan*—Old carpets, wool mixed with goat hair or camel hair—no feature made of Kelim ends.

(*p*) *Rest of Europe*—These are as English and French in foundation.

Dates woven into rugs—

Some rugs are dated and it is always important to look carefully over each rug to see if it is. From these dated rugs we are able to judge the ages of other rugs as it is of course, a first-class guide.

Dating (Arabic numerals)

DATES WOVEN INTO RUGS

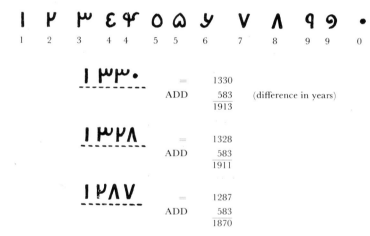

The Moslem year begins on the 16th July, A.D. 622 (the day of Mohammed's flight from Mecca to Medina). The Moslem year is also eleven days shorter than our own. Rather than complicate the issue use the *583 year* difference which is a simple guide to the approximate date.

Afghanistan

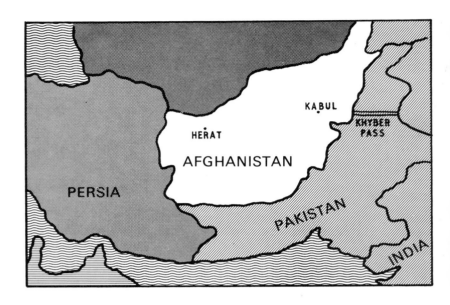

GENERAL:

Eleven and a half million population, approximately 60 per cent are tribesmen, a large percentage of these are wild and live in mountainous ranges of which most of the country consists. It is difficult to believe that in 1969, they still raid caravans, as in centuries gone by.

The chief road to the capital, Kabul, is through the Khyber Pass from the east and Herat from the west—Herat is believed to have at one time been the capital of the old Persian Empire and many old carpet looms were discovered there in the early part of this century. These looms dated back to before the twelfth century. The main wealth of the country lies in the enormous flocks of sheep (flat-tailed) and humped cattle, which roam the hills and valleys.

Owing to the mountainous terrain, donkeys and camels are still used for transport. The climate is ideal for rearing the long fleece sheep, its wool being excellent for carpet weaving.

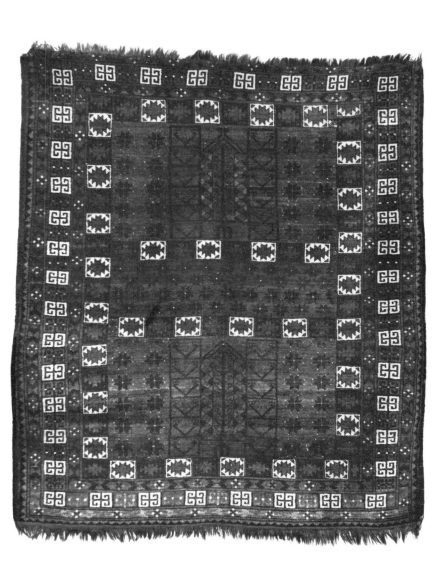

2. Afghan Hatchlie Prayer rug; 7 ft. × 4 ft. 10 in. Tawny red ground with deep reds, blues and browns.

27

When asked to describe an Afghan carpet, you either say a golden or red carpet with a repetitive octagonal design woven across its field. Let us first deal with the golden. These were originally red carpets which have been chemically treated, removing the red, and leaving a golden, brown colour in its

3. Afghan rug; 6×5 ft. Pale red ground with dark reds, beige and browns.

place. This treatment has been going on since the early 1920s. When it was first tried, many thousands of rugs and carpets were ruined because they were burnt by the acid used. Thirty years ago a neutrallising process was perfected and thousands of carpets have been treated every year without ill-effect, so far. The reason for such treatment was, because in the early 1920s French furniture was very fashionable and interior designers and decorators needed a simple, pastel design. Afghans were very cheap, so the cost was comparitively low, if they were ruined by the chemical treatment. As the treatment proved successful over the years, other more expensive Persian rugs were tackled. It is possible to tell if such treatment has taken place by folding the pile and looking for red roots or a pinkish uneven tinge to the fawn.

Today, merchants have been trying to get weavers to use golden wool supplied by them, so as to save the cost of chemical treatment. So far, however, very few have been woven, as old traditions die hard and some weavers are very superstitious and believe a change of colour will bring bad luck.

The quality of Afghans, as with all Orientals varies quite considerably, in fact, from one extreme to the other. I have seen rugs so fine and so stiff, that it has been impossible to fold them, they had to be rolled or laid flat.

The use of camel hair is not unusual, on close inspection the fields of many beige ground rugs are found to be of camel hair.

The Persian knot is the most common used, but it is not unusual to find a rug woven with a Turkish knot.

The design is made up of octagonal medallions (guls), each tribe having its own particular shape. The Afghan is nearly always a true octagonal, the sides being squared off, *unlike the Turkoman which have curved sides or pieces protruding from their guls*. The guls in the Afghan are not joined, like most of the Bokharas which use a thin blue line. (See diagrams of guls.)

Key

1. *Designs*	Look for free standing guls (elephant's foot), not joined in any way.
2. *Knot*	Persian, although the Turkish knot is found to be used.
3. *Dyes*	Dark red, light red, light brown and dark brown grounds with blue-green, natural and sometimes yellow.
4. *Wool*	From medium quality to good. Goat hair is used in many rugs.

5. *Side cords*	Single, double, or treble usually flat and heavy depending on the fineness of the carpet or rug.
6. *Ends (warp)*	Wool or goat hair and wool.
7. *Weft*	Wool or goat hair and wool.

Belouchestan

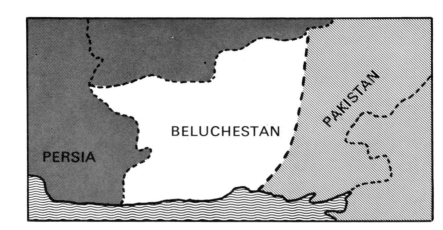

MASTER KEY TO BELOUCHESTAN

GENERAL

At first glance to the layman, all Belouchestan rugs look dark and uninteresting with few other colours save black, dark brown, plum, beige and a little natural. That might well be so by today's weavers, but, I can assure you, there are Belouchestan rugs in some of the world's finest collections, and quite rightly so. Old rugs, well made, have the most elaborate 'Kelim' ends ever seen on rugs. Their design may be primitive and stylised, but it is subtle. The dyes are well balanced to give the best effect in a limited range. The weave is from coarse to the extremity of fineness. The finest are classified as Meshed Belouche (which have a four stranded, check pattern flat cord —see *Side cord* section).

They are often mistaken for Afghanistans, but a closer look reveals that the Belouchestan colours are like plain chocolate and the Afghanistans like milk chocolate.

4. Belouchestan Prayer rug. Camel ground with reds, browns and blues. Note the wide cords.

Modern Belouchestan rugs have been made with merserized cotton and rayon, which makes them look like silk; the designs staying the same. These can be confused with the new Anatolians, which use the same materials, the difference being that Anatolians have a Turkish knot.

Key

1. *Designs*	Semi-geometrical with stylised 'Trees of life', square-ended prayer rugs, hands are often seen either side of the niché, fancy 'S' designs, or flower heads on Kelims.
2. *Knot*	Persian.
3. *Dyes*	Dyes are limited to plum red, brown, black, blue, beige (light khaki) and natural, on rare occasions yellow and white cotton.
4. *Wool*	Generally good, although poor quality has been used.
5. *Side cords*	Double flat cords in average Belouchestan and check pattern, as cord diagrams show.
6. *Ends (warp)*	The majority of old rugs have wool and goat hair, on modern rugs cotton is used.
7. *Weft*	The same as applicable to ends.

N.B.—Regarding 'Kelim' ends, as explained, they are always one of the delightful features of Belouchestans and it is a great pity that modern rugs are made with plain cotton fringes.

BELOUCHE *(plates 4 and 5)*

Key

1. *Designs*	Simple semi-geometrical designs.
2. *Knot*	Persian.
3. *Dyes*	Dark and heavy.
4. *Wool*	Good quality to poor.
5. *Side cords*	Double flat or else check pattern on meshed Belouché.
6. *Ends (warp)*	Wool and goat hair, fawn and brown look.
7. *Weft*	Wool and wool and goat hair mixed. 'Kelim' ends finely woven in delightful designs; 'S', flower or zig-zag motifs.

5. Belouchestan rug. Dark reds, browns and blues on a camel ground. Note the wide cords.

Caucasus

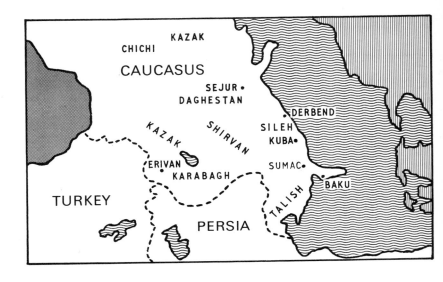

GENERAL:

Caucasia, the land which lies between the Black Sea and the Caspian Sea—where legend has it, is, 'The Valley of the Golden Fleece', live many different peoples, Georgians, Tartars, Cossacks, Circassians and Armenians, all with their own culture and religions. From time to time, one reads about the long-lived Caucasians—a place where many men live to over a hundred and some to 160 years of age.

The Caucasus mountains practically stretch across the width of the country, and the lower slopes are ideal for sheep rearing. Their rug designs are geometrical as the mountain slopes which are about them, powerful, magnificent and yet a picture of tranquillity. Each people having its own particular type of geometrical design.

MASTER KEY TO CAUCASIANS

To learn the name of every Caucasian is a study of a lifetime. Try to put every type of Caucasian into the fourteen classifications, which I have listed and you will not be greatly amiss; if you feel later that you demand greater knowledge, a reputable dealer in antique rugs would most certainly help.

5. Rumanian Kelim Hunedoare district.

6. Baku (Hieler). Dark blue ground with cone design. Note the medallions which are set in a fine line surround.

6. Koula. *Circa* 1800. Sold at Sotheby's, £800 (1969).

7. Chichi rug.

At first glance, all Caucasians look alike with their geometrical designs, but a closer look at your *keys* will soon alter that, showing their tell-tale peculiarities. Try to pick out their differences and using them well will certainly surprise you.

The name Armenian is often associated with Caucasian rugs. This was due to the fact that in the twelfth and thirteenth century the Armenians wanted freedom of religion and they moved from Eastern Turkey to the Caucasus.

Some of the Armenians were without doubt great weavers

Key

1. *Designs*   All designs are geometrical, except the Kara-

36

bagh, with its floral motifs; the Dragon Kuba with its dragons; the Talish with its plain field; the Baku (Hieler) with its cone field; the tapestry type Soumac (verné) and Sileh Kelims; the Dagestan with its Prayer rug or diagonal stripes; the Sejur with its 'X'; the Chi-Chi with its band border and medallion field; the Erivan with its cotton foundation; the Kazak with its long pile and large, bold, primitive design—eleven out of fourteen classifications with outstanding differences.

2. *Knot* All have Turkish knot.

3. *Dyes* All the dyes used by the Caucasians were vegetable until 1890, when a deep orange coloured wool was introduced. This was bought or bartered for by the weavers, as to dye to this colour was impossible (the nearest colour was a pomegranate rind). Unfortunately, it was either fugative or faded, which has ruined many hundreds of rugs. Fortunately, some weavers only used a little to highlight designs. Taking advantage of this knowledge, we know that when we see this orange in a rug, we are able to date it, often, as 1890. In the 1920s the use of aniline dyes in Erivan had taken a hold, and most rugs woven since that date have man-made dyes.

Apart from these points, the Karabagh has the most vivid purple-red, or else has been chemically washed, and has a black and buff look.

4. *Wool* Short pile on all the rugs, except the Kazaks, which have long lustrous wool, and Erivans which have a medium length dryer type of wool.

5. *Side cords* Except for the Kazaks, which have a double and sometimes a treble stranded woollen cord, and the Dagestan which sometimes has a cotton, double flat cord, the Caucasians all have a double wool cord.

6. *Ends (warp)* Apart from the Erivan using cotton, the remaining weavers used either wool or wool and hair.

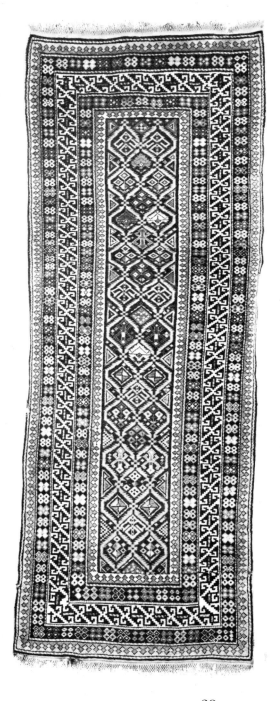

8. Daghestan runner;
12 ft. × 3 ft. 9 in. On a blue
ground.

7. *Weft*	Apart from the Erivan using cotton, the remaining weavers used either wool or wool and hair.

9. Daghestan Prayer rug; 5 ft. 9 in. × 3 ft 3 in. On a white ground with pale blue and dark blue borders. *Circa* 1820.

10. Close-up of Daghestan back.

BAKU *(Hieler) (plate 6)*

Baku, Hieler (sometimes called Shirvan) is an easy to recognize rug by its field of cones (feather Saraband) motifs and its one, two or three stripped medallions. Usually woven with dark blue fields but pale blue, although rare, have been seen.

Key

1. *Designs*	Many borders, cone field with medallions set in fine line surround.
2. *Knot*	Turkish.
3. *Dyes*	Indigo, pale green and blue.
4. *Wool*	Good, resilient.
5. *Side cords*	Double flat wool.
6. *Ends (warp)*	Wool.
7. *Weft*	Wool.

CHI-CHI *(plate 7)*

A fine type of Northern Caucasian rug, much sought after by collectors and woven on an indigo or medium blue ground, which is covered by very small geometrical medallions as many as 100 in the centre panel of 5 ft. × 2 ft.

Key

1. *Designs*	The main border always has small diagonal bands separated by small '+', a very noticeable feature.
2. *Knot*	Turkish.

11. Derbend rug; 9 ft. ×4 ft. 6 in. *Circa* 1830

3. *Dyes*   Strong and good quality dyes.
4. *Wool*   Good quality, short and tough.
5. *Side cords*   Double flat wool.
6. *Ends (warp)* Wool.
7. *Weft*   Wool.

DAGHESTAN *(plates 8, 9 and 10)*

Normally seen in Prayer rugs, but also made in trellis or diagonal stripe centre runners. It is not usually a very fine rug, but has a charm of its own.

12. Erivan; 5 ft. 5 in. × 3 ft. 5 in. *Circa* 1948.

Key

1. *Designs*	Either trellis or diagonal stripes.
2. *Knot*	Turkish.
3. *Dyes*	Strong in every way but good balance.
4. *Wool*	Short, tough and good.
5. *Side cords*	Cotton—double strands natural or wool.
6. *Ends (warp)*	Wool.
7. *Weft*	Cotton when cords are cotton, wool when cords are wool.

DERBEND *(plate 11)*

On average a dark looking rug, often mistaken for Shirvan. Although austere, they are rather eloquent rugs. Large Derbend carpets are often seen, up to 19 ft. × 7 ft.

Key

1. *Designs*	These vary, but the general look is dark, although light Derbends have been made.
2. *Knot*	Turkish.
3. *Dyes*	Mostly dark in colour.
4. *Wool*	Good quality.
5. *Side cords*	Double or treble flat in wool.
6. *Ends (warp)*	Wool.
7. *Weft*	Wool, also one of the most obvious characteristics is the Soumac Kelim in blue on the ends, which is the best way to confirm its identification.

ERIVAN *(plate 12)*

The modern Shirvan as it is called, only dates back to the 1920s, and many thousands of these rugs are produced now per year. Copies of most designs like their next door (Ardebil) are unlike other Caucasians because of their use of cotton weft and warp, also aniline dyes which tend to be flat in comparison.

Key

1. *Designs*	Although difficult to define, they are generally copies of Shirvans.
2. *Knot*	Turkish.
3. *Dyes*	Flat aniline dyes.
4. *Wool*	Good, but pile is longer than most Shirvans.
5. *Side cords*	Cotton which is unusual for Caucasians.
6. *Ends (warp)*	Cotton which is unusual for Caucasians.
7. *Weft*	Cotton which is unusual for Caucasians.

43

KABISTAN and *(Kuba Kabistan)* *(plate 13)*

Names of the finest types of Caucasians with Kufic borders and Rams' horns. Designs always well balanced. Most rugs were made prior to 1900, and sizes of 12 ft. × 5 ft. to 14 ft. × 6 ft. are often seen.

Key

1. *Designs*   Small and intricate geometrical designs.
2. *Knot*   Turkish.
3. *Dyes*   Soft and dark blue ground and madder red Kufic borders.
4. *Wool*   Short pile and good quality.
5. *Side cords*   Double stranded wool.
6. *Ends (warp)* Wool.
7. *Weft*   Wool.

13. Antique Kabistan rug; 6 ft. 9 in. × 4 ft. 2 in. Depicting rams horns, ancient keys and camels with a Kufic main border and fine Barber's pole border. *Circa* 1840.

KARABAGH *(plates 14 and 15)*

The most southern of the Caucasians, it lies on the border of Persia. The rugs are recognized by two main points. One the combination of geometrical and floral designs and the other is the use of a very vivid purple-red, once seen never forgotten.

44

This colour was so overpowering that, in the 1920s these rugs were chemically washed removing the red and leaving a black and buff look, which was and still is an excellent colour for types of furnishing.

14. Karabagh; 12 ft. × 4 ft. 9 in. On a vivid red ground. Dated 1809.

15. Karabagh; 9 ft. 6 in. × 4 ft. 9 in. Dark blue medallions set into a vivid purple-red ground.

1. *Designs*	Large or small floral designs mixed with geometrical.
2. *Knot*	Turkish.
3. *Dyes*	Vivid purple-red, black grounds, strong colours.
4. *Wool*	Very good, tough wool.
5. *Side cords*	Double flat wool.
6. *Ends (warp)*	Wool and wool and goat hair.
7. *Weft*	Wool.

KAZAK *(plates 16 and 17)* ; colour plate.

The most nothern of the Caucasians with enormous designs in comparison with the rest of the Caucasians. They have long pile and a heavy double weft. Some designs have names to describe them, such as, Sun Burst, Bird, or Crab. Sizes above 9 ft. × 7 ft. are rare.

16. Kazak. Close-up of back. Note heavy wefts.

Key

1. *Designs*	These are large and bold with only three borders, one main and two small on either side. Other than already mentioned, most

	have large, almost elephant's foot medallions, which are full of design and colour.
2. *Knot*	Turkish.
3. *Dyes*	Madder grounds are the most common, blue-green and all strong colours.
4. *Wool*	Long, lustrous, good quality wool.
5. *Side cords*	Double and treble stranded.
6. *Ends (warp)*	Wool or wool and goat hair.
7. *Weft*	Nomadic rugs use a black wool and goats' hair mixed, average rugs use wool.

17. Kazak. Close-up of front. Note texture and fringes.

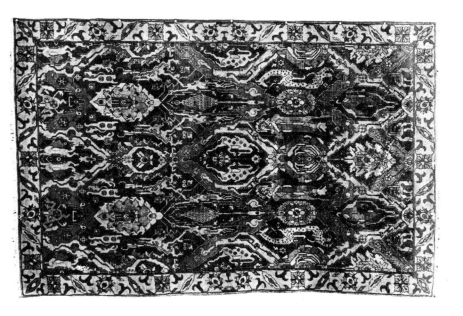

18. Dragon Kuba. Sixteenth century.

KUBA or *(Dragon Kuba) (plate 18)*

Sometimes called Armenian carpets, Kubas date back to the thirteenth century and were made by the Armenians in the Caucasus. These found their way into Italy in the thirteenth and fourteenth centuries and are often seen in the paintings of the period.

Key

1. *Designs*	This consists of a large type of trellis with sections of geometrical palmettes or stylised dragons.
2. *Knot*	Turkish.
3. *Dyes*	Usually woven on a madder and blue ground with striking colours.
4. *Wool*	Short, tough and resilient.
5. *Side cords*	Double flat wool.
6. *Ends (warp)*	Wool.
7. *Weft*	Wool dyed red.

49

SEJUR *(plate 19)*

Made in the south Caucasus, this is one of the most appealing Caucasians, usually woven on a natural ground but can be seen on red and blue. The design consists of three large 'X' and a white and blue latch hook border, which makes it very outstanding and simple to distinguish.

Key

1. *Designs*   The large 'X' with semi-geometrical floral designs in between.

2. *Knot*   Turkish.

19. Sejur; 6 ft. 6 in. ×4 ft. 7 in.

7. Sunburst Kazak; 8 × 5 ft.

3. *Dyes*   Brown always seem to be worn out, other colours are gay.
4. *Wool*   Good quality, short pile.
5. *Side cords*   Wool, double flat.
6. *Ends (warp)* Wool and wool and goat hair.
7. *Weft*   Wool.

SHIRVAN *(plate 20)*

More numerous than any other Caucasian rug. In fact, rugs are often labelled Shirvan for want of a better name. Generally medium to fine quality, but not good enough to warrant Kabistan or Kuba.

Key

1. *Designs*   Small geometrical patterns.
2. *Knot*   Turkish.
3. *Dyes*   Dark blue and strong reds.
4. *Wool*   Short and tough.
5. *Side cords*   Double stranded wool.
6. *Ends (warp)* Wool.
7. *Weft*   Wool.

20. Shirvan rug; 5 ft. 6 in. ×4 ft. 4 in. *Circa* 1850.

51

8. Persian Polonaise; 6 ft. 9 in. × 4 ft. 9 in. *Circa* 1640. Sold at Sotheby's, £6,600 (1969).

SILEH

Sileh are made in a similar manner to the Soumac not knotted but woven and consisting of two parts sewn in the middle, with large S-shaped figures in square panels throughout. They are all made *circa* 1800.

Key

1. *Designs*	Large square shaped 'S', on a blue and madder ground.
2. *Knot*	Tapestry weave as in Soumac.
3. *Dyes*	Bold colours.
4. *Wool*	Good quality.
5. *Side cords*	Double stranded wool.
6. *Ends (warp)*	Wool and wool and goat hair.
7. *Weft*	Wool, weft is actual pile and design.

21. Soumac. Close-up section of back. Note chain stitch.

SOUMAC *(Verné) (plates 21–23)*

Soumac, these get their names from the Caucasian town of Shemakha. However, they are mostly made in Derbend. They are the easiest to distinguish, for they have a flat stitch and leave loose ends at the back (as would be seen on a tapestry or needlework, see plates Chain Stitch, which show back and front). The design usually consists of three main medallions,

22. Soumac. Close-up section of front. Note chain stitch.

geometrical in shape. The main colours are dark red ground, dark blue, green and yellow.

Key

1. *Designs*	Geometrical, large medallion rugs (Verné, small panel designs).
2. *Knot*	Tapestry weave (see plates Chain Stitch).
3. *Dyes*	Strong, bold colours.
4. *Wool*	Good quality.
5. *Side cords*	Double strand wool.
6. *Ends (warp)*	Wool and hair.
7. *Weft*	Wool weft is actual pile and design.

TALISH *(plate 24)*

This Southern Caucasian runner with its dark blue and some-times madder red field, is an easy rug to recognize. Sometimes one will also see in the field a man and a woman primitively drawn or a small repetative design.

Key

1. *Designs*	Note the main border which has a repeating design which is always common to all Talish rugs. These are the four dice shapes and the circular motifs separating them.

2. *Knot*   Turkish.
3. *Dyes*   Strong, indigo and madder.
4. *Wool*   Good quality.
5. *Side cords* Double flat wool.
6. *Ends (warp)* Wool.
7. *Weft*   Wool.

23. Soumac; 8 ft. 6 in. × 5 ft. 6 in. On a pale madder ground.

24. Talish Runner; 9 × 3 ft. Indigo field. *Circa* 1800. Note the main border with its circular motif and four dice.

China

China history dates back to 5000 B.C., and by 2000 B.C. they were making pottery of elegant shapes. They had discovered bronze and were making fine, sacrificial vessels, which can be seen in the British and other museums today.

It is difficult to believe that the first carpet weaving was late seventeenth century, as fragments of this date are the only ones which have survived. Today, two facts must be considered, which are:

(a) The Russian carpet which was found in the Alti mountains, which border on Mongolia and China, and is dated 500 B.C. (see section on Russian carpets).

(b) In A.D. 1256 Halagu Khan, grandson of Genghis Khan, brought 100 families of Chinese artisans and engineers into Persia. Surely the Mongol weaving of 500 B.C. must have spread its wings by this time, taking into consideration the fact that the Khans had conquered from China to the Black Sea.

All the eighteenth and most of the nineteenth century up to 1860, carpet designs remained the same. The general texture being coarse with double or several wefts used in between each row of knots. Designs incorporated the Chinese symbols of religion, the arts, superstitions or the simple type of fretwork medallion.

In the late nineteenth century, carpet weaving took on a new look—weavers started to use the single weft, therefore, carpets became much finer. Designs were influenced by the American and European markets, which demanded at first simple designs and then a new type, which had to look so typically Chinese that the layman would have no difficulty in recognising it. Hence the Chinese temples, elephants, cranes and oxon which appeared. By the mid-1920s the height of the pile was increased from $\frac{1}{4}$ to $\frac{3}{4}$ in.

In the early 1930s, once again, a new process and a new look appeared—the chemically super-washed carpet, with pile an inch in height and a look of a French Savonnerie carpet in design. America and Europe imported thousands of them. Today, they remain the same, only the designs have become more intricate. In 1954, America closed its doors to Chinese imports and the Chinese found that the demand for the super

25. Chinese Kansu Pillar rugs. *Circa* 1800.

Chinese started to wane—and not wanting to flood the expensive market—they started to make cheaper super-washed carpets, $\frac{5}{8}$ in. pile, then $\frac{3}{8}$ in. pile, and finally semi-washed, which had the same look but could be sold for one-third or half of the price of the super-washed.

When buying a Chinese carpet have a good look around and check the quality; most carpets have a specification sewn on the back. If not, ask the salesman, he will be able to check his invoice, which will certainly classify the rows of knots and the height of pile. *Do not* be fooled by seeing two carpets which look the same, and one is half the price of the other.

26. Chinese rug. *Circa* 1965. *See also col. plate. Circa* 1950.

Key

1. *Designs*   Before 1860—incorporating the Chinese symbols of the arts, religions, superstitions and the simple type of fretwork medallions;
From 1860 to 1930—Chinese temples, elephants, cranes and oxon;
From 1930 to 1969—super-washed self-embossed French designs with carved pile.

58

27. Chinese Saddle cover. *Circa* 1780.

2. *Knot*	Persian.
3. *Dyes*	Rugs woven prior to 1860 are of vegetable dye and the majority up to 1900, but after that date to 1930, I would estimate that 50 per cent are aniline dyes, and since 1930 all are aniline dyes.
4. *Wool*	The wool in the early carpets is good but shaggy, from 1860 it seemed in most cases to improve, in carpets made since 1930 the wool is good.
5. *Side cords*	Before 1860—cotton double cords; 1860 to 1930—single cotton; 1930 onwards—heavy woollen cords.
6. *Ends (warp)*	Cotton throughout all periods.
7. *Weft*	Prior to 1800—from two to five strands were used; 1800 to 1860—from two to three; 1860 onwards—one weft strand only was used.

Footnote

Has chemical washing Chinese carpets affected them in any way?

(*a*) No noticeable deterioration has taken place.
(*b*) Slight fading of the wool tips has taken place.

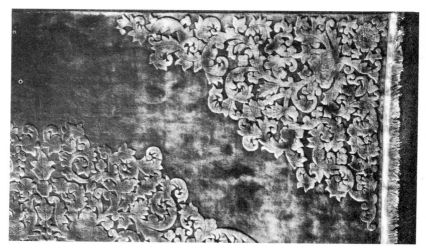

28. Chinese Super washed self-embossed. *Circa* 1956.

Egypt

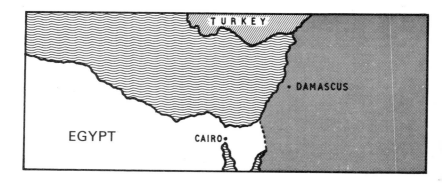

MASTER KEY TO EGYPT

GENERAL:

Egyptian history dates back to 6000 B.C. (pre-dynastic). Owing to the hot rainless atmosphere in its burial pits and rock temples, many of the ancient arts have been preserved, even dresses worn by ladies 2000 B.C. have survived intact. Coptic textiles (Kelims) were found with simple designs of animals, however, the first fragment of carpet, as we know it today, was found in Fostat, ninth century A.D.

29. Cairene style Egyptian rug. Sixteenth century.

There are four important periods of carpet weaving in Egypt, and they are as follows:

    PERIOD I—Mameluke carpets; 1400 to 1517
    PERIOD II—Ottoman carpets; 1517 to 1600
    PERIOD III—Brussa carpets; 1600 to 1700
    PERIOD IV—Egyptian carpets; from 1700 until today.

Let us deal with the two important facts, which are:
(a) cotton was not introduced into Egypt until 1760 by Mehemet Ali;
(b) all carpets have Persian knots, before and after the Ottoman invasion.

In 1474, the Venetian traveller, G. Barbaro, said that Tabriz carpets were better than those made in Cairo, he was referring to the coarse, semi-geometrical design carpets, the Mamelukes.

The next period was the Ottoman, here two designs evolved:
    i. the copies of Ispahan, Tabriz, Kirman;
    ii. the Cairene carpets, Damascene style (see Damascene style, under Turkey—general) and compartment carpets.

The third period is the Brussa. Seventeenth-century designs were more open floral and like open Damascene work. The carpets all being woven on a silk weft and warp. In the fourth period, carpet weaving fell away, as they were not able to compete with other countries, and during the last century, only reversable Kelims of cotton have been made.

Dates	Periods		Weft	Warp	Pile
1400–1517	I	Marmeluke	Wool	Wool	Wool
1517–1600	II	Ottoman (*Cairene style*)	Wool	Wool	Wool
1600–1700	III	Brussa	Silk	Silk	Wool
1700–1950	IV	Carpets	Wool	Wool	Wool/cotton
		Kelims	Cotton	Cotton	Cotton

Key
1. *Designs*   See periods.
2. *Knot*   All Persian, all cotton Kelims have reversable tapestry weave as Bessarabians.
3. *Dyes*   Mostly dark reds, brick, dark green, browns. Cotton tends to fade.

30. Egyptian seventeenth century Brussa carpet (Damascene).

4. *Wool*	Dry, but strong wool, cotton in Kelims strong.
5. *Side cords*	Fine single, practically none existant.
6. *Ends (warp)*	Wool/silk/cotton—see chart.
7. *Wefts*	Wool/silk/cotton—see chart.

England, Ireland and Scotland

MASTER KEY TO ENGLAND, IRELAND AND SCOTLAND

GENERAL:

A date has never been established as to when British carpet weaving commenced, so I have compiled the known facts to date and from these we will apply observations, comments and the key.

ENGLAND A.D. 1225 Edward I brought his new Queen Eleanor of Castile to England and rugs were hung from the windows, of which some were Spanish. Edward I was on the crusades in 1274, and he must have compared the Asia Minor rugs with the Spanish brought over by Eleanor.

A Guild of carpet makers existed in Paris, *circa* 1300. The most important point I would like to establish at this stage, is that early carpets were used on tables and not on the floor, as the early paintings prove. They may have been listed as table covers, which, of course, could be difficult to trace; therefore, one must not be hood-winked by seeing household accounts and inventories listing rushes and straw for the floors, and believe carpets never existed until later.

ENGLAND A.D. 1450 the first piece of hand made carpet with a Turkish knot was made to cover a chair, by whom it is not known—this can be seen today in the Victoria and Albert Museum (London). (The date has been disputed owing to the fact that hand knotting might not have been known so early, but that could be ruled out, and the date stand). These chair covers have been named 'Turkey Work', of which many pieces have been seen and dated sixteenth century.

ENGLAND A.D. 1520 Cardinal Wolsey received from Sebastian Giustinian, the Venetian Ambassador, sixty *Damascene* carpets via *Antwerp*. These are listed on British records, as sixty *Turkey* carpets without description or size.

IRELAND 1530 Sir Robert Rothe brought out of Flanders weaver of carpets and tapestries, and he tried to start a trade

31. English Morris carpet. 1880.

in such goods from his home town, Kilkenny.

SCOTLAND 1539 in the wardrobe inventory of James V were many pieces of Turkey carpet, some made of silk.

ENGLAND 1570 an English Heraldic carpet, property of the Earl of Verulam, dated 1570 with E.R. above the Royal Arms, either side in separate panels are the arms of the *Borough of Ipswich* and those of the family Harbottle. (The Harbottle family were shippers).

ENGLAND 1579 Messrs. M. Richard Hackluit of the 'Middle Temple' sent a Mr. Humblethorne to Persia to learn the secrets of dyeing and weaving.

ENGLAND 1584–1585 Dates woven into the carpets of (Sir Edward Montague) now Duke of Buccleuch.

65

32. English Needlework rug; 6 ft. × 3 ft. 4 in. Yellow field with donkey brown border. *Circa* 1920.

ENGLAND (India) 1600, the year the East India Company was established in Lahore. There was also a Royal Carpet Factory in the palace of the Moghul Emperor, Akbar, which was set up twenty years prior, when Persian weavers were brought to Lahore.

One of the first carpets woven for an Englishman, was for Sir Thomas Roe, James I's Ambassador at the Moghul court (1615–1619). Then, five other carpets were made to order and in 1633 were completed. Four were for Sir John Wolstenholme (Director of the East India Co.) and one to Robert Bell, which was presented by him to the Girdlers Company in 1634. It bore the company's coat of arms. (This carpet is still in the company's possession today, and, I believe, will be shown at the Victoria and Albert Museum (London) in the autumn of 1970. The make-up and name of these carpets are important, and must not be confused with the British carpets; these are classified as *Indo-Ispahan* as the weavers were Persian by origin. The designs are certainly of Persian style, except for the coat of arms. *All the wefts and warps were cotton, the knots Persian.*

ENGLAND 1600, 1602, 1603, 1614, 1620, five more carpets bearing these dates:
1. *1600*—a fragment believed to be the property of Lord Verulam;

66

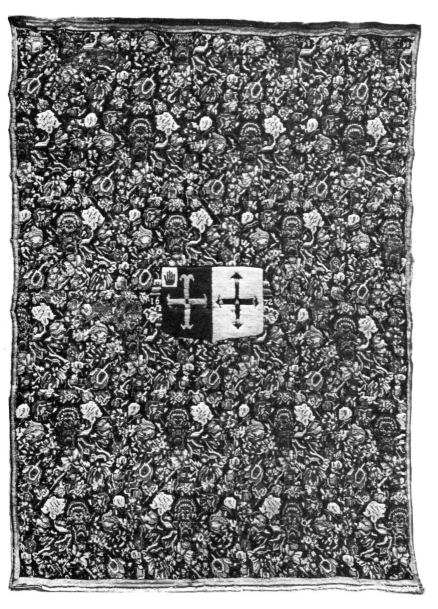

33. English. Dated 1672. Small shield with arms of Molyneux impaling Rigby. Note either side of small shield date 16–72 and shield bears the 'Bloody Hand' of Ulster—The badge of a Baronet.

10. Elizabethan needlework table carpet; 9 × 6 ft.

2. *1602*—the property of Bridget, Countess of Bedford;
3. *1603*—the property of Sir Edward Apsley;
4. *1614*—the property of Sir Hamilton Westrow Hulse;
5. *1620*—the property of Lord Sackville.

ENGLAND 1672 the Heraldic carpet with a centre coat of arms of the Molyneux impaling Rigby and the shield bearing the 'Bloody hand of Ulster' is probably the most British of all the carpets, resembling the close floral designs of the early English 'Turkey Work'.

One final carpet, mentioned in a letter to Sir Robert Sidney dated 29th November 1602 from a Mr. Brown, who writes, 'I have bought a Turkey carpet for my Lord Bergavenny, seven Dutch ells long'.

OBSERVATIONS

Apart from the two carpets belonging to the Duke of Buccleuch, which have silk wefts, all the others are consistent in make-up, having hemp or flax weft and warps, also the Turkish knot. Some designs were copies of the Ushaks (Turkish), others were more English in make-up.

WHERE WERE THEY MADE?—From the information, they could have been made in England, Ireland or Flanders. When further information comes to light, which will most certainly happen one day, it will be by some letter of complaint about size, colour or coat of arms to a weaver of table covers in Turkey work.

ENGLAND EIGHTEENTH CENTURY, the first record is of a small factory in Wiltshire, established 1701, the Wilton Royal Carpet Co., and after that date not until the great influence of the French carpets began when the families of weavers, the Hugenots and the Passavans, left France and in the year 1750 set up weaving in Westminster and Fulham. At that period there were, in England, only two well-known weavers, one Thomas Moore of Moorfields, and a Thomas Whitty of Axminster. Carpets were of French influence at first, and later the Adams brothers produced their own designs. In some cases, they made carpets and ceilings to match, as in Harewood Hall and many other stately homes. The establishment of carpet factories soon spread, Axminster—Devon 1759; Brintons—Kidderminster 1783; Woodward Grosvenor—Kidderminster 1790; Cooke Sons—Yorkshire 1795; and reversable wool carpets from Champion & Co.—Gloucester 1778.

SCOTLAND—James Templeton—Glasgow 1839.

34. English carpet belonging to Sir Hamilton Westrow Hulse. Dated 1614.

IRELAND—1898 Killybegs, the home of the Donegal carpet, which still makes hand-made carpets today.
ENGLAND—William Morris Carpets 1878.

Observations of the eighteenth and nineteenth century carpets
Carpets woven by the Hugenots and Passavans in Exeter and elsewhere have white woollen wefts and warps, while the others have jute, flax or hemp wefts, with woollen warps.
   All knots are the Turkish type.

69

35. English Axminster. *Circa* 1820.

Designs are English and French, although the Donegals are subdued in colour. The Morris carpets have designs, colours and styles of their own, almost an 'English' type Persian.
ENGLISH NEEDLEWORK (Carpets and Rugs), once again no trace of any beginning, just sixteenth and seventeenth century examples of fine work, having initials of weavers or tapestry factory marks, traced back to either Sheldon tapestry works or

70

Mortlake works. By the middle of the sixteenth century, needlework was a part of the routine of life by ladies of the manor, and we find great numbers of chairs and pole screens covered in fine work. In 1880, Cambridge and Birkenhead workrooms started making needlework carpets, rugs and pole screens, and many of them can be seen today.

In the 1920s, a Mr. Pontremoli, started making heavy needlework carpets in Paddington. There were two ladies of Mount Street, London, W.1., who made many fine rugs. Apart from all these, we are never surprised to find early needlework carpets, which have been made in convents; one of the earliest of these that I have seen, was dated 1764.

OBSERVATIONS (see colour plate Elizabethan needlework.)

To ascertain the age of a needlework rug, one need only compare it with early dated pieces, for colour, texture and general appearance. The subjects can be very misleading. There are always exceptionally fine examples of sixteenth, seventeenth and eighteenth century pieces to be seen in textile museums all over the world, which are one's best measure.

Key

1. *Designs*	The early carpet weavers copied the designs of the Turkish carpets and from 1600 onwards, a type of European-Persian design evolved. From 1670 the motifs became more 'chintz'. From 1750 the influence of France showed throughout the designs. From 1830 hand machine-made carpets of all designs were manufactured. (The Lahore carpets are not included as they are, of course, Indian).
2. *Knot*	All have Turkish knot.
3. *Dyes*	Early carpets had brown/blue/red or blue-green grounds, while later fields were varied as were the designs.
4. *Wool*	All wool of a heavy Turkish-type—good quality.
5. *Side cords*	Heavy woollen cords of between two to six strands.
6. *Ends (warp)*	Early carpets all had hemp or flax. After 1750 the use of wool was introduced by the French weavers of Axminster and Thomas Moore of Moorfields. Nineteenth century carpets varied, some of flax and some of wool, however, William Morris (1878) was one of the

71

36. Irish from Donegal;
11 ft. 1 in. × 4 ft. 7 in.

first to use cotton (the only other example was an experimental piece of carpet made by Mr. Wentworth Buller 1885).

7. *Weft*

Apart from the Duke of Buccleuch's carpets having a silk weft, all the other early carpets have hemp or flax. After 1750, the use of woollen weft started, but in the nineteenth century, jute or hemp is to be found (William Morris (1878) used jute or hemp). Most of the 'Kelim ends' were woven with a small narrow *web*, this can be seen turned back or frayed out to make a small fringe.

Finland

FINLAND
• NAANTALI
• HELSINKI

MASTER KEY TO FINLAND

GENERAL:

The suggestion that Finland was once the home of the Laps and that the Finns are of the Finno-Ugrian group, which is related to the Estonians and Hungarians certainly seems to ring true as far as the textiles are concerned. However, from the twelfth to the end of the eighteenth century, Finland was subjugated to Sweden and today both languages are still taught in schools. The first point is to clarify the word 'Ryijy' (Rya)— it is a Finnish word and it was the name of a Kelim tapestry (not reversable—but like a Soumac). These were used for either horse cloths, sledge rugs, coverlets, wall tapestries or rugs, most probably in that order. It is a tough, all wool, colourful rug. There is also evidence that it was originally a part of the maiden's 'bottom drawer', which she had to make and it was the custom for the couple to stand on it while the wedding ceremony was in progress, (these have a boy and girl design in the centre, sometimes holding hands). As well as this, there is the fact that Rya rugs are a part of death benefit inherited under what is known as the 'Widow's Bed' (goods which she inherits automatically).

The first evidence of the Rya is an inventory of 1495, from a

37. Finnish dated 1835

convent near Naantali. The next, also from the same district reads, 'to include eleven Ryijy rugs', 1549.

The true Rya looks like a Bessarabian Kelim, except that it is more of a tapestry and has loose ends at the back; that is why I said originally, that there was some attachment to that part of Europe. However, the actual weaving of these rugs is either carried out by families or their employees.

In the eighteenth century and possibly before, a long pile rug evolved, made with a Turkish knot but with the Spanish method of using several weft strands in between each row of knots (easy to distinguish between the two, because of the Spanish knot). The designs are semi-geometrical, stylised flowers and zig-zags, which are often dated—see illustration.

Rya rugs, as we know them today, are long, shaggy pile rugs, which come from the Scandinavian countries.

Key

1. *Designs*	Early Ryas are like the Bessarabians (Rumanian), eighteenth and nineteenth century rugs, see illustration.
2. *Knot*	Turkish knot or tapestry weave, quality from 60 to 300 knots to the square inch.
3. *Dyes*	All vegetable until this century.
4. *Wool*	Good quality, tough wool.
5. *Side cords*	A fine flat cord with Kelims, and flat end in eighteenth and nineteenth century rugs.
6. *Ends (warp)*	Are of all wool, until the nineteenth century when cotton and hemp was introduced.
7. *Weft*	As Ends (warp); a good point to watch is the use of several weft strands (up to six or seven).

France

MASTER KEY TO FRANCE

GENERAL:

Although France has existed since the fifth century, it was not until the ninth century that it became the 'Empire of Charlemaine'. It was Louis IX (1226–1270) known as Saint Louis, who developed the arts. Gothic was at its height, cathedrals

38. A fine Beauvais rug, Aubusson type; 6 ft. 8 in. × 6 ft. 3 in. Woven with gold metallic thread, making up the trellis ground and outer edge, with a central medallion focusing on a bouquet of flowers. On a natural ground with varying shades of pink and powder blues. *Circa* 1840.

were built all over Europe and the univer~ity in Paris (the Sorbonne) was the centre of learning.

At this period, a Guild of carpet makers existed, but unfortunately their products have not been found, probably because everything was either sold, destroyed, lost or taken as booty in the 100 years war (1337–1453). The sixteenth century in France was marred by the religious wars between the Roman Catholics and the Protestants (Huguenots) and it was not until 1598, when Henry IV issued the Edict of Nantes, which granted the Protestants freedom of religion, that France was at peace

with herself, and started to prosper. In 1603, Jean Fortier and
Pierre Dupont boasted of their knowledge of carpet weaving,
so in 1606, Henry IV gave Dupont an Atelier in the Louvre.
The carpets woven, marked the beginning of a new era of
carpet weaving.

Louis XIV (1643–1715) was not satisfied by the slow progress of carpet weaving, so he appointed Simon Lourdet, a
pupil (a relative of the Dupont family), to start the Savonnerie
carpet factory in 1626. The word Savonnerie is derived from
the fact that the factory was once a soap works on the bank of
the Seine, at Chaillot, Paris. Two stipulations were made, one
was that sixty workhouse children would have to be employed
(aged ten to twelve years old), and second that the Royal

39. A late Louis XVI Aubusson carpet; 21 ft. 5 in. × 18 ft. 11 in. (Collection René Fribourg).
Photo courtesy of Sotheby and Co.

painter (permier), Charles Lebrun, to Louis XIV would visit the factory once a month to supply, inspect and control the designs. Seventeenth century France had become the admiration of the world and the arts had been allowed to develop to the full. Four looms were set up to make carpets 33 ft. wide. Carpets were supplied to the King of Siam, and the King of Denmark. By the end of the seventeenth century France had overspent and Louis XIV foolishly used the Protestants as scapegoats. He revoked the Edict of Nantes, and within a few years, 250,000 Protestants were to leave France never to return. They took refuge in Germany, the Netherlands, Switzerland, the American colonies and England, each country benefiting from their great skill in textile manufacturing.

During the beginning of the eighteenth century France purchased Pondicherri, a town in India (relinquishing it in 1954) and carpet weaving was started on a small scale. Indian carpets in French designs, which are much sought after today, were produced there. The first of the eighteenth and nineteenth century, and up to the present, hand-made carpets are being manufactured in the same style as the early carpet designs, relating to the contemporary architecture, and the more modern from 1850–1950, being more relaxed with ribbons, and bows and without the strong bold medallions.

Aubusson—In the eighteenth and nineteenth centuries
Tapestry looms were converted and used for making large and small tapestry carpets, which are known today as Aubussons, with similar designs and colourings as the Savonnerie, of their periods.

Key

1. *Designs*	Although the very early designs of 1610 were completely floral, they soon took on a look of boldness and designs were made to match ceilings of palaces.
	1850 to the present day, the style has become more relaxed with ribbons and bows.
2. *Knot*	Turkish.
3. *Dyes*	Bold, almost violent colours, which today have mellowed.
4. *Wool*	Always found to be first class, heavy and lustrous. Early silk carpets were made.
5. *Side cords*	Heavy stranded, all wool.
6. *Ends (warp)*	All wool in the early carpets, but in the eighteenth century carpets flax was laid bet-

	ween every two strands of warp.
	18th century Aubusson—made of wool.
	19th century Aubusson—made of cotton.
7. *Weft*	Wool was used in the early carpets until the nineteenth century after which cotton and flax can be found. (Kelim ends are turned back or frayed out to make a small fringe.)
	As Aubusson are tapestry, the weft is the pile and made of wool.

Iceland

MASTER KEY TO ICELAND

GENERAL:

The first settlers came to Iceland in A.D. 874 and it remained independent until 1263, when it became a part of Norway. In 1381, Iceland with Norway came under the Danish kings, but when Norway was separated from Denmark in 1814, Iceland remained a Danish possession until 1944, when the ties were severed and a republic was proclaimed.

Iceland is known more for its embroideries, than small rugs, as such, and these are used as coverlets, or hangings.

The illustration shows an Icelandic embroidered bedcover, made for Pall Bjornsson, born 1621, died 1706. The Gothic writing is as follows, the two top lines and both sides read: 'Asleep and awake we truly belong to God himself whether you give us death or life we will not seek help from others; we thank you for Jesus Christ'. The two lines at the bottom read: 'The light of the sun will soon disappear and the dark night will begin once more: light of our souls, be with us forever'. Words from the hymn printed in Holar in the north of Iceland in 1589. Pall Bjornsson's name can be seen in the two bottom centre panels: PALL BJ in the left centre, and ORSS/N in the right centre panel.

Key

Pile, weft and warp are all wool, colours are yellow ground with reds, blues and greens.

Today, in Iceland, hand-made rugs are still made in the homes as they were hundreds of years ago.

40. Icelandic embroidered bedcover; 5 × 3 ft. Made for Pall Bjornsson, born 1621 died 1706.

India, Kashmir and Nepal

MASTER KEY TO INDIA, KASHMIR AND NEPAL

GENERAL:

The first information, which comes to light is that in the eighth to ninth century, Faristan weavers from Southern Persia settled in Bombay, unfortunately no trace of their work can be found.

From the ninth to the middle of the fifteenth century little is known; mid-fifteenth century Prince Shahi Khan, son of the ruler of Kashmir founded the carpet Industry and it was producing carpets until the eighteenth century, after which the lack of demand and other factors closed down the workshops (by the middle of the eighteenth century carpet weaving in Europe was at its zenith).

A.D. 1580 The Moghul Emperor, Akbar, brought carpet weavers from Persia and set up a Royal carpet workshop in his palace at Lahore. In the south carpets were being woven in

41. A normal chain stitch rug produced in Kashmir.

42. An extra fine chain stitch rug produced in Kashmir.

Warangal. In 1600, the East India Carpet Co. was established in Lahore and soon after workshops were set up in Amritza, Agra and Dehli.

From Lahore came some of the world's finest carpets of the seventeenth century, the Indo-Ispahans. The first of these to arrive in England was made for Sir Thomas Roe, the ambassador to James I at the Moghul court (1615–19) having his arms thereon. Then the next five carpets; four for Sir John Wolstenholme, (Director of the East India Co.) and one for a John Bell, all of equal quality. The most important of these, is that of John Bell, as it can be seen today at the Girdlers Hall, London; there is no doubt that it is one of the finest complete surviving examples of the Lahores or 'Indo-Ispahans', (being made by Persian weavers) and the early designs were copies of the Kirman, Kashan, Herat, and, of course, Ispahan.

Later in the seventeenth century designs, were bold and elegant and pure Indian in style. In 1679 weaving workshops were set up in Ellura and a few years later in Musulipatam. There were some twenty cities weaving carpets and their products can be seen in the Indian palaces today.

In the eighteenth century there was a decline, brought about by the weaving centres of Europe developing to meet their demands, and people bought at their convenience (even if dearer). However, the French bought Pondicherri in 1702 (giving it up in 1954) and a small workshop, which produced the most delightful *Indo-French* designs in the latter part of the

43. Indian rug made 1930–1969.

82

11. A section of a Shiraz Kelim.

eighteenth century and all the nineteenth century, which are much sought after today.

By the first-quarter of the nineteenth century, very little weaving was being carried out, however, a group of Germans re-opened workshops in Amritzar and set up a new workshop in Srinigar, which produced carpets for nearly a century, until the company got into financial difficulties after World War I (1919) and were bought out by the East India Company. In 1840 another factory was opened in Amritzar by a family of weavers from Kashmir. Soon after Kandahar, and Mirzapur started opening workshops and by 1867 Mirzapur was the largest weaving centre in India; these carpets won acclaim for their design and texture. Also a Messrs. Mitchell & Co. of Kashmir had developed quite a good name for fine carpets.

44. Indian rug made 1930–1969.

Agra jail set up a workshop and started to produce some of the finest of the world's carpets; these to the astonishment of many, are found in the majority of palaces and stately homes all over the world but are unfortunately sometimes erroneously called Persian.

By the twentieth century, Indian carpets became popular, not only because they were cheaper, but also people required other alternatives to the ornate Persian and Turkish carpets. Another point was, that China was having internal trouble, so very little was produced, and at that time these were the only

12. Antique Bergama; 5 ft. 4 in. × 4 ft. 10 in. Prayer rug.

45. A fine Indian Kelim; 7 ft. 4 in. × 4 ft. 5 in. Yeraoda district.

alternatives. However, factories sprung up all over India and in the 1920s the Mirzapur was a *Household* name.

After World War II, because of demand, a cheaper carpet was produced, and as always it began a downward trend in quality until in 1952 it reached rock bottom with a 12 ft. × 9 ft. carpet selling (retail) for £16—$45 U.S. This, of course, gave Indian carpets a very bad name, which was such a pity after so many years of first class workmanship. However, reputable dealers kept the quality up and today you have fine selections of either mill or hand spun wool in a good range of designs.

The cotton *Dari*, a reversable cotton drugget, mainly made in Yeraoda, Shikarpur, Hyderabad and a few other towns used either to sleep on or as cheap floor covering, can be delightful in many ways. They have semi-geometrical Persian designs, just plain stripes or sometimes animals woven into them.

The procedure, if you wished to have a Dari made, would be to approach a Dari weaver, arrange the design, give him the materials and pay him for his labour when he has finished or by arrangement. Daris have become very fashionable in Europe and large ones are cut up to cover patio furniture, as apart from being hard-wearing, its faded look is very pleasing to the eye.

46. Indo-Ispahan rug. *Circa* 1620.

Kashmir—chain-stitch

During this century, very fine chain-stitch rugs and carpets have been made in Kashmir. These are made of the finest wool and are very decorative, see illustrations.

Nepal

In the Himalayan mountains only rugs are produced, their size is usually 6 ft. × 3 ft. and the designs are a type of Chinese —with geometrical dragons on yellow and blue grounds.

Key

1. *Designs*   The designs of the sixteenth and seventeenth century were Persian in every way and the true Indian influence took place in the middle of the seventeenth century, about the time the Taj Mahal was near completion. However, owing to the fact that either the East India Co., the French or the Germans controlled the majority of carpets, designs had to suit their varying markets and were of course, in some cases, adulterated. Modern designs are either spray corners or Aubusson. Dari and Nepal, as explained in the general text of India.

2. *Knot*   All are Persian (Sehna), chain-stitch on Kashmir.

3. *Dyes*   Most colours are similar to the Persians—but the one which is most outstanding is the deep green, with its bluish-yellow glow. This green is certainly one of the deciding factors of your *identification*.

4. *Wool*   Kashmir and Srinigar wools are of a very soft texture (probably too soft). Agra, Amritzar and most of the other centres have a tougher, dryer and more hard-wearing type of wool (Agra produced many, all-pile heavy cotton carpets). Today, mill spun wool is imported from Australia. Daris are made of all cotton (Kelim reversable weave).

5. *Side cords*   Very heavy single overcast cords, wool on woollen carpets, and cotton on cotton carpets.

6. *Ends (warp)* All cotton, Daris all cotton, silk carpets all silk.

7. *Weft*   All cotton, no feature is made of the Kelim ends. Jute is used in some of the cheaper carpets. Daris all cotton.

47. Indian 'Agra'. *Circa* 1850.

48. Indian Fremlin carpet. Seventeenth century.

Morocco

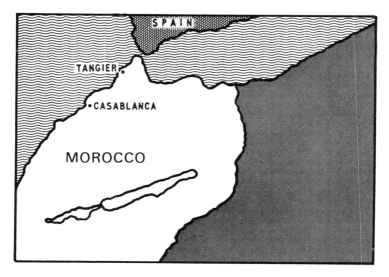

MASTER KEY TO MOROCCO

GENERAL:

Morocco is known and called in arabic 'The Farthest West', which dates back to the Ottoman invasion 1517, when it was the western most place of that empire. In the early years, the Moors controlled Spain, until A.D. 1212 and in fact they held the Kingdom of Granada until 1492. From the fourteenth century, Spanish carpets were woven and I am sure weaving must have taken place in Morocco. Unfortunately, only fragments of fifteenth century rugs have been found, and complete carpets of the eighteenth century are seen in most museums.

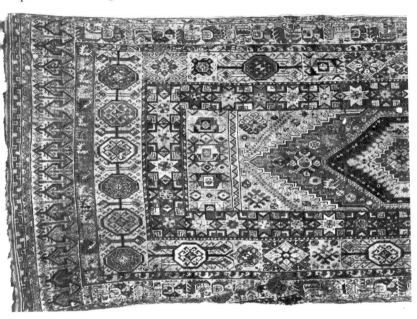

49. Morocco. *Circa* 1800.

The eighteenth century pieces are usually soft, mellow colours with very loose weave. The nineteenth century and early twentieth century rugs are strong, almost garish in colour. Today, a good selection of hand-made rugs, using only grey, brown and natural wool are made.

Key
1. *Designs*   Early rugs were very ornate, geometrical

	designs; twentieth century rugs have become more simple geometrically.
2. *Knot*	Persian.
3. *Dyes*	Early rugs used light mauve, generally pale colours. Late nineteenth century and early twentieth century dyes were crude in bright reds and yellows.
	Rugs today have natural grounds with browns and greys.
4. *Wool*	Good wools on early rugs; late nineteenth and early twentieth century used poor wool; today, good wool is used.
5. *Side cords*	Double flat cords of wool.
6. *Ends (warp)*	Wool and goat hair until late nineteenth century, early twentieth century—then cotton.
7. *Weft*	Wool and goat hair until late nineteenth century, early twentieth century—after that cotton.
	Wefts are usually made with three or as many as seven strands between each row of knots, which gives an appearance of a loose weave and immediately identifies it.

Norway

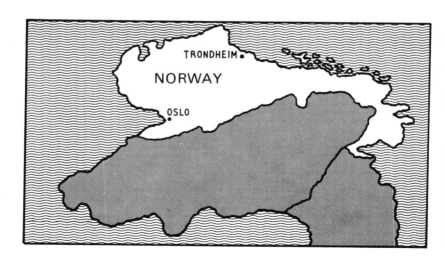

GENERAL:

Norwegian history dates, as with Iceland, back to *circa* A.D. 872 and their histories are linked together.

Norwegian early works are very rarely seen and it is believed that very little was produced before the seventeenth century. The early work was primitive and quaint, designs were simple and pleasant. Their tapestry-type rugs were sometimes of religious origin and subjects.

The first illustration shows a Norwegian seventeenth century tapestry depicting the ten Virgins. The subject is taken from St. Matthew's Gospel, chapter 25, verse 1. 'Then shall the Kingdom of Heaven be likened unto the ten Virgins, which took their lamps and went forth to meet the bridegroom, and five were wise and five were foolish. They that were foolish took their lamps and took no oil with them, but the wise took oil in their vessels with their lamps'.

50. A rare Norwegian tapestry; 5 ft. 9 in. × 4 ft. 7 in. *Circa* 1600. Depicting the ten virgins.

The second illustration shows a Rya tapestry rug or wall hanging made *circa* 1625, with an interesting design of stylised spear-heads.

Hand-knotted rugs and Kelims are made today in Trondheim. These are made-to-measure. Also, of course, you still have the Rya rugs which are made in the homes and are used either for the walls, or floors, (for definition of Rya—see *Finland*).

51. Norwegian. *Circa* 1635.

Pakistan

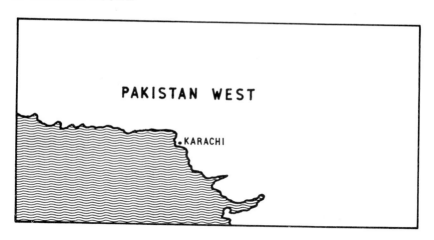

PAKISTAN WEST

.KARACHI

MASTER KEY TO PAKISTAN

GENERAL:

The creation of Pakistan was on the 14th August 1947, a Muslim state, before that it was part of British India and the Indian states. Therefore, its history of carpets is as old as India, dating back to the eighth and ninth centuries, when the Faristan tribes settled in the area and started carpet weaving. However, I am only dealing with the new carpets and rugs which have been produced since 1947.

From small beginnings, weaving only rugs in designs of Bokhara (elephant's foot), French Aubusson, Chinese Caucasian, Persian hunting rugs and Turkish prayers (Bokhara being the most popular), they gained a foothold on the world market. Then, they produced rugs with a chemical lustre, which looked like silk—later silk carpets and rugs were produced.

Today, 10,000 looms are producing carpets and rugs, and a new loom to make carpets up to 27 ft. × 16 ft. has just been installed.

Key

1. *Designs*	No real traditional design, all copies of every country.
2. *Knot*	Persian (Sehna).
3. *Dyes*	A mixture of vegetable and aniline dyes, cherry reds tend to be very bright, blues dull.

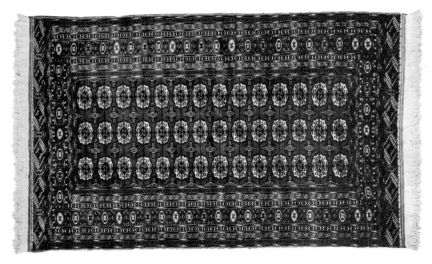

52. Pakistan; 6 ft. 6 in. ×4 ft. 2 in. Copy of a Tekke Bokhara (Turkestan). Note the over elaboration.

4. *Wool*	The wool tends to be very soft, in fact, possibly too soft and can be easily parted with the thumb, which is a good way to recognise them. The silk is heavy and dull.
5. *Side cords*	These are single overcast and usually the same material as the pile.
6. *Ends (warp)*	Made of white cotton, and white silk on silk rugs.
7. *Weft*	Cotton weft or silk weft on silk rugs, no feature is made on Kelim ends.

Point to note : Bokhara (Turkestan) rugs *never* use cotton weft or warp, as do Pakistan rugs.

Persia (Iran)

GENERAL :

Persia has been known as Assyria, Media, Persia and now Iran and dates back to 2,000 years B.C. The first information of carpet weaving is an extract from an Arabian manuscript regarding a carpet, made for the King of Persia, Chosroes I

94

53. Ardebil Persian. Dated 1540. The inscription on the bottom reads:
'I have no refuge in the world other than thy threshold. There is no place of protection for my head other than this door. The work of the slave of the Threshold. MAQSUD of KASHAN in the year 946.'

95

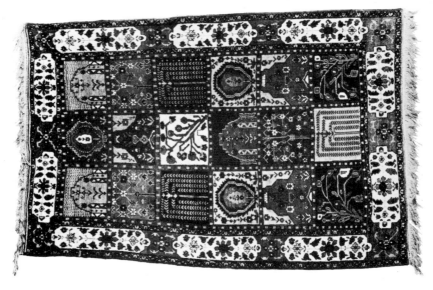

54. Persia Bakhtiari; 7 ft. × 4 ft. 8 in. *Circa* 1860.

(A.D. 531–579). It was called the winter or spring carpet of Chosroes, and it was made of silk, gold, silver, semi-precious and precious stones and the design was of a garden carpet. The borders represented flower beds and in the flower heads were stones of red, blue, yellow, green, amber and white, a small stream was represented by clear crystal. The carpet was truly magnificent, was it an 'Arabian Dream'?—as so many have said. My views are: (a) they understood carpets at that time—and (b) they had nothing to gain by such a tale.

It was not until 1063 that the country, under Seljukes, became the core of civilisation; the days of Omar Khayyam (1063–1123). In 1218, Persia was once again conquered, this time by Ghengis Khan and in 1256 his grandson brought 100 families of engineers and artisans to Persia—was it to teach or to learn? Two facts follow this event, the first is that Marco Polo on his return to Venice (1295) remarked that the carpets of Tabriz were finer than those of India; and secondly, there is a carpet in the Kaiser Frederic Museum in Berlin which has Chinese motifs and is ascribed as Persian made in 1320. Not until the sixteenth century, when the Ardebil carpet (1540) was produced and the Shah Abbas period began (1586–1628), did the second golden age of Persia commence, during which the world's finest carpets were produced.

Key
1. *Designs*

Dividing the country up you have:

   i. *Western area designs*—Fereghans, Sehnas, Zieglers, Mahals, Hamadans, Malayers, Mousuls, Karajars, Gorevans, Herizs, Mirs and Bidjars (which are a group of similar designs, either heavy and bold or distinguishable by their individuality).

55. Persia Fereghan rug; 6 ft. 2 in. × 4 ft. 1 in.

	ii. *Central area designs*—Kashans, Sarouks, Teherans, Ispahans, Qums. (Fine typical Persian designs.)
	iii. *Southern area designs*—Kirmans, Yezds are rose-floral, Shirazs and Afshars are geometrical.
	iv. *Eastern area designs*—Mesheds (Birjand), dark and similar to the central area designs.
2. *Knot*	Apart from Tabriz, Herat, Gorevan, Bidjar, Heriz and the few Kurdish tribes on the western border all knots are Persian.
3. *Dyes*	Three main groups:
	i. *Western*—colours, terracottas, brown, natural and pale and dark indigo.
	ii. *Central*—red, deep reds, brick and rose.
	iii. *Eastern*—dyes take on a darker look, Meshed/Birjand have the colours similar to the old Indian and Kashmir rugs with the dark Indian green, unlike any Persian green.
4. *Wool*	Three main groups:
	i. *North-western*—dry, hard, tough yarn (sometimes mixed with hair).
	ii. *Central and southern*—good quality wools.
	iii. *Eastern*—poor to good quality wools.
5. *Side cords*	Three main groups:
	i. the tabriz with its double flat cords
	ii. in general overcast cords are used.
	iii. the Shiraz cords which have either bands of different colours or a mixture of two colours.
6. *Ends (warp)*	Generally cotton, although the Kurdish tribes use camel hair and the Shiraz district use a mixture of hair and wool. Most modern rugs of wool pile have cotton except very fine Nians which have silk and, of course, most silk rugs are woven on silk although cotton can be used.
7. *Weft*	Mostly cotton and undyed. The exceptions are as follows: Shiraz—red weft of wool or wool and hair; Kashan, Mahal and fine Kirman—pale blue weft. Kelim ends, Shiraz fancy designs. Tabriz sometimes have four lines of wool in check pattern in two colours. Kashan sometimes have two lines of wool in

13. Rava Kirman carpet; 15 ft. 10 in. × 10 ft.

56. Antique Fereghan saddle cover, blue ground, pale green border, a most rare piece.

check pattern in two colours.

ARDEBIL *(plate 53)*

Ardebil, home of the famous carpet, lies at the north-west edge of Persia, twenty miles south of the Caucasian border, where a modern type of rug, of Caucasian design, is woven with a Turkey knot.

Key

1. *Designs*	Modern rugs copies of mostly Caucasians.
2. *Knot*	Turkish.
3. *Dyes*	Tend to have Persian colours rather than Caucasian.

14. Josuagan carpet; 15 ft. 8 in. ×8 ft. 4 in. *Circa* 1800. Sold at Sotheby's, £4,200 (1969).

4. *Wool*	Heavier than Caucasian.
5. *Side cords*	Cotton, natural colour.
6. *Ends (warp)*	Cotton.
7. *Weft*	Cotton.

BAKHTIARI *(plate 54)*

The Bakhtiari tribe are of Kurdish origin and roam the areas from Shiraz to Hamadan. The features of their carpets and rugs are similar to the Hamadans, but they are usually softer in texture.

Key

1. *Designs*	Usually in a tile pattern, each tile having alternate designs—see illustration.
2. *Knot*	Persian.
3. *Dyes*	Strong and bold.
4. *Wool*	Good to medium quality.
5. *Side cords*	Heavy, single overcast.
6. *Ends (warp)*	Cotton.
7. *Weft*	Cotton.

BIDJAR

Bidjar is from the town of Bidjar. The pile is of heavy, lustrous wool, medium length tied with a Sehna knot. The features are similar to the Sarouks (but not as fine) and the truly Kurdish rugs made in the district. They are usually very heavy for their size.

Key

1. *Designs*	Bold and heavy.
2. *Knot*	Persian or sometimes Turkish.
3. *Dyes*	Strong blues, lime greens, tomato reds.
4. *Wool*	Heavy, lustrous wool.
5. *Side cords*	Overcast in wool.
6. *Ends (warp)*	Cotton natural.
7. *Weft*	Cotton natural.

FEREGHAN *(plate 55)*

Fereghan is from the plains of Fereghan. The older pieces have the Sehna knot but in later specimens the Ghiordes knot is also common. The pile is short and of good wool. The colours are usually predominantly red and blue, though in older pieces a notable amount of light green is used. The field is mostly covered with a repeating design, such as Herati, and the cutting off of the field by straight lines normally occurs at the corners. There are from 65 to 400 knots per square in.

100

57. An old Heriz; 16 ft. 9 in. × 12 ft.

Key

1. *Designs*	Small design of flying sword fish facing each other.
2. *Knot*	Persian.
3. *Dyes*	Blues, madders and pale green.
4. *Wool*	Short and fine.
5. *Side cords*	Overcast in wool.
6. *Ends (warp)*	Cotton.
7. *Weft*	Cotton, sometimes pale blue in colour.

GOREVAN

Gorevan is a town situated below Tabriz beside Lake Urima and carpets made there have a Ghiordes knot and are coarsely woven with approximately thirty to forty knots per square in. The colours are usually copper to copper-red field, dark blue and fawn. The design is often one large geometrical medallion with smaller similar medallions within.

Key

1. *Designs*	Large, medallion carpets. Like Heriz (plate 57).

2. *Knot*   Turkish.
3. *Dyes*   Madder reds, blues, naturals and a little green.
4. *Wool*   Heavy, coarse and tough.
5. *Side cords*   Overcast in wool.
6. *Ends (warp)* Cotton.
7. *Weft*   Cotton.

58. Persia Herat carpet. *Circa* 1850.

HAMADAN *(plate 59)*

Hamadan carpets are named after the city. They are of medium texture, and made with camel hair hexagonal designs. Rather large, plain borders are usually woven when making runners, which are in abundance. Ghiordes knot is used. The main colour is camel. Finer rugs are classified as Sehna-Hamadans. They have many more colours and are usually soft, thin and pliable.

A fine example of a sturdy Hamadan-Kurdish rug is shown in the plates.

Key

1. *Designs*	Heavy and semi-geometrical.
2. *Knot*	Turkish (Ghiordes), or Persian knot.
3. *Dyes*	Dark blues, strong madders, pale yellow (saffron).
4. *Wool*	Heavy wool mixture of goats hair and camel hair.
5. *Side cords*	Overcast heavy.
6. *Ends (warp)*	Camel or goat hair mixed with wool or cotton.
7. *Weft*	Camel or goat hair mixed with wool or cotton.

HERAT *(plate 58)*

Herat, although now united with Afghanistan, was under Persian rule during the flourishing days of Persian carpet weaving, and had the reputation of making the best carpets in Persia. The design is composed entirely of palmettes with floral stems and cloud bands. The peak period for weaving was the seventeenth and early eighteenth centuries. The chief colours are dark blue, red, white, green and yellow. Carpets are still woven today in Herat. Ghiordes knot.

Key

1. *Designs*	See plate 58, for a perfect example.
2. *Knot*	Turkish.
3. *Dyes*	Dark indigo, heavy green and deep reds.
4. *Wool*	Short and tough.
5. *Side cords*	Overcast in wool.
6. *Ends (warp)*	Cotton.
7. *Weft*	Cotton.

HERIZ *(plate 57)*

Heriz, a town some forty miles south-east of Tabriz, where

carpets similar to the Gorevan are made. The Heriz is usually much finer in quality of wool and stitch. Silk rugs are usually exceptional in quality.

Key

1. *Designs*	Large medallions with geometrical look, clear and fine.
2. *Knot*	Turkish.
3. *Dyes*	Madders, blues, pale greens and natural.
4. *Wool*	Short, tough and lustrous.
5. *Side cords*	Overcast in wool.
6. *Ends (warp)*	Cotton.
7. *Weft*	Cotton.

ISPAHAN *(Josuagan)* *(plate 62)*

In the city of Ispahan in the sixteenth and seventeenth centuries the proud inhabitants used to say that, 'Ispahan is half the world'. The city was one of the world's most important centres, since at least the time of the Achamenians. It has two of the most beautiful buildings in the world, the Mosque of the Shah and the Mosque of the Sheik Lutfulla facing each other, neither finding an equal in any other place on earth. There is also the fascination of the shaking minarets and the superb old bridges, which span the Zayanded river.

Ispahan, Josuagan are famous carpets of the sixteenth and seventeenth century. Today, carpets are still woven in these districts. The old carpets had approximately 100 to 160 knots per square in. In the last 100 years, rugs have been made much finer, the chief designs being blossoms, cloud-bands and palmettes as so often seen in rugs of the sixteenth and seventeenth centuries. The colours are varied and numerous. There have been early silk carpets reputed to have come from these districts which have had as many as 600 Sehna knots to the square in. woven with metallic (silver and gold) thread. Modern rugs woven in the outskirts of Ispahan in the Nian district have pride of place in the weaving of Iran today.

Illustrated is a fine Ispahan rug with prayer arch depicting four birds of paradise. This is a good example of the weaving and designs in the late nineteenth century. Also shown is an Ispahan rug, size 7 ft. 10 in. × 4 ft. 11 in., a new rug of exceptional quality woven in the factory of Sarrafia in the early 1950s on a white ground, the small borders being pale blue.

Key

1. *Designs*	Typical examples illustrated.
2. *Knot*	Persian.

3. *Dyes*	Brick very common in borders and medallions.
4. *Wool*	Soft, lustrous pile of medium length (some silk rugs).
5. *Side cords*	Fine, single cord, overcast, Type A, wool/silk.
6. *Ends (warp)*	Cotton—sometimes silk on fine rugs.
7. *Weft*	Cotton or silk.

59. Hamadan Runner; 12 × 4 ft. Note wide outside borders.

60. Heriz Silk; 5 ft. 11 in. × 4 ft. 5 in.

KARAJA *(plate 63)*

Karaja, a village north of Heriz not far from the Caucasus, is renowned for its runners and also small rugs, which are not unlike the Heriz but are rather more geometrical. Their pile is usually clipped much shorter. Not to be confused with the village of Karaj, west of Hamadan.

Key
1. *Designs*   Geometrical mixed with semi-floral (stylised).
2. *Knot*   Turkish.
3. *Dyes*   Heavy dyes, mostly dark colours.
4. *Wool*   Heavy and short.
5. *Side cords*   Overcast in wool.
6. *Ends (warp)* Cotton.
7. *Weft*   Cotton.

KASHAN *(plates 64 and 65)*

Kashan made in the city of the same name, is one of the finest types of Persian carpet. The fine texture and thick pile make the rug stiff; often the sides curl. Graceful designs are used, with curved medallions and well-drawn floral borders. Sehna knots from 160 to 600 per square in.

Plates show a very fine example of a silk Kashan prayer rug, tree of life design, made in the early part of the twentieth century.

Key
1. *Designs*   Tree of life, centre medallion, and all over designs.
2. *Knot*   Persian.
3. *Dyes*   Not unlike the Teheran but not so dark.
4. *Wool*   Short lustrous wool pile, silk fine and short also part silk.

61. Nian; 7 ft. 10 in. × 4 ft. 11 in. Woven in Mamori factory. *Circa* 1950.

Above
62. Ispahan; 7 ft. 10 in. × 4 ft. 11 in. Woven in Mamori factory about 1950.

Right
63. Karaja Runner; 18 ft. 8 in. × 3 ft. 2 in.

Below
64. Kashan; 7 ft. 2 in. × 4 ft. 6 in. Silk and wool pile tree of life design Prayer rug. *Circa* 1930

5. *Side cords*	Single overcast, Type A of wool.
6. *Ends (warp)*	Cotton or silk.
7. *Weft*	Cotton or silk (*cotton dyed blue*), old rugs natural.

KIRMAN *(plates 66 and 67)*

The remotest city of Persia, it lies on the edge of the Lute desert. It was a thriving town when Marco Polo passed through. Much of its fame still exists, through its produce or exquisite silks, embroideries, and fine carpets.

Entirely surrounded by desert, it is geographically the centre of Iran, the centre of the Zoroastrian religion. In the fourteenth century, Marco Polo termed it as, 'A good and noble city' : and the seventeenth century French traveller, Tavernier, said, 'It is true to the gallantry of its country'.

Kirmans, sometimes called the carpet of the roses, are mostly of soft, delicate colouring with very naturalistic designs incorporating cypress trees, vases, animals and birds. They have a Sehna knot and are usually extremely fine. The old Kirman is usually thin and has from 200 knots per square in. The modern Kirman has a thick pile and the design is sometimes of a skeleton type—woven without the usual borders—but not as fine. Silk rugs are rare.

Plates show a carpet, depicting the story of Laila and Majnoo, is a good example of the delicate weaving associated with Kirman, and also a Kirman rug, size 7 ft. × 4 ft., which is a typical example of a fifty year old Kirman.

Key

1. *Designs*	Fine, floral.
2. *Knot*	Persian.
3. *Dyes*	Bright rose, soft blues, and an abundance of light grounds.
4. *Wool*	Medium length to long and lustrous.
5. *Side cords*	Overcast wool.
6. *Ends (warp)*	Cotton.
7. *Weft*	Cotton.

KERMANSHAH *(plate 68)*

Kermanshah, one of the relatively new cities of Persia. Ancient ruins are to be found in the neighbourhood, the most important of these being the inscriptions of Darius the Great, on the rock face of the Bisotun mountain. Although Kirman is 700 miles away, their designs are sometimes similar. They are made with a Sehna knot and are usually very fine.

65. Kashan rug; 7 ft. × 4 ft. 6 in. On a red ground. *Circa* 1930.

66. Kirman rug; 7×4 ft. Depicting the story of Laila and Majnoo, natural ground with rose and pale green borders. *Circa* 1900.

KELIMS

SEHNA or PERSIAN KELIMS *(plate 74)*

Woven in designs not unlike the Sehna rug (later examples in semi-floral designs) and are usually of exceptional quality.

The warp is usually of wool. The weft is the actual design and is made of wool. (See plates showing their make-up.)

SHIRAZ KELIMS; colour plate 5

Often mistaken for Caucasians, are very attractive and are

111

67. Kirman carpet; 13 × 10 ft. Made for the American market. *Circa* 1930.

woven on the same principle as the Sehna Kelim but much coarser and the designs are geometrical. Warp is a mixture of wool and goat hair, usually very dark. The weft, which makes up the design, is of wool.

MAHAL

Mahal, from the district of Sultanabad looks like large designed Fereghans, the difference being that they are usually soft, coarser and are sometimes called the Persian equivalent to the 'Turkey Carpet'. The larger carpets have scrolling semi-floral patterns, rather scattered. They are known to have Sehna and Ghiordes knots, approximately 40 to 50 per square in.

68. Kermanshah; 20 ft. 10 in. × 10 ft. 6 in.

Key

1. *Designs*	Mostly copies of Fereghans, but coarser and more open in design.
2. *Knot*	Persian or Turkish.
3. *Dyes*	Dark blues, madders and natural.
4. *Wool*	Coarse.
5. *Side cords*	Overcast in wool.
6. *Ends (warp)*	Cotton.
7. *Weft*	Cotton, *dyed blue*.

MALAYER *(plate 69)*

Malayer is a town near to the city of Hamadan, where two main types of rug are woven. One type of carpet resembles the

113

Hamadan and the other the Sarouk. This is understandable with Hamadan being twenty-five miles to the north and Sarouk thirty miles to the east. The knots are Turkish. The rugs are usually marketed in Hamadan.

Key
1. *Designs*   Cross between Sarouk and Hamadan.
2. *Knot*   Turkish.
3. *Dyes*   Lean towards Hamadan, not Sarouk.
4. *Wool*   Short and tough.
5. *Side cords* Overcast.
6. *Ends (warp)* Cotton.
7. *Weft*   Cotton.

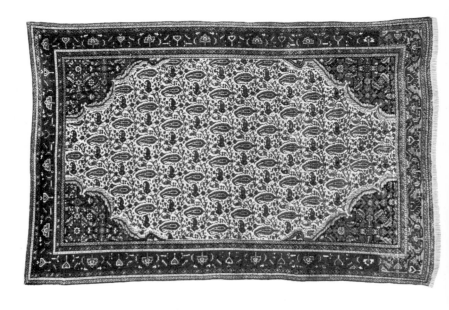

69.   Malayer rug; 6 ft. 4 in. × 4 ft 3 in. Natural ground, pale blue border with dark blue corners.

MESHED *(Khurasan, Turkbuff, Birjand) (plate 70)*
The capital city of the province of Khurasan. Since the ninth century this has been a place of pilgrimage, for its great, gold domed Mosque shelters the tomb of Imam Reza, the most venerated saint of the Shia Moslems. The city, which is situated in the north-east of Persia, attracts the tribesmen of

114

15. Gigim carpet; 9 ft. 3 in. × 5 ft. 10 in.

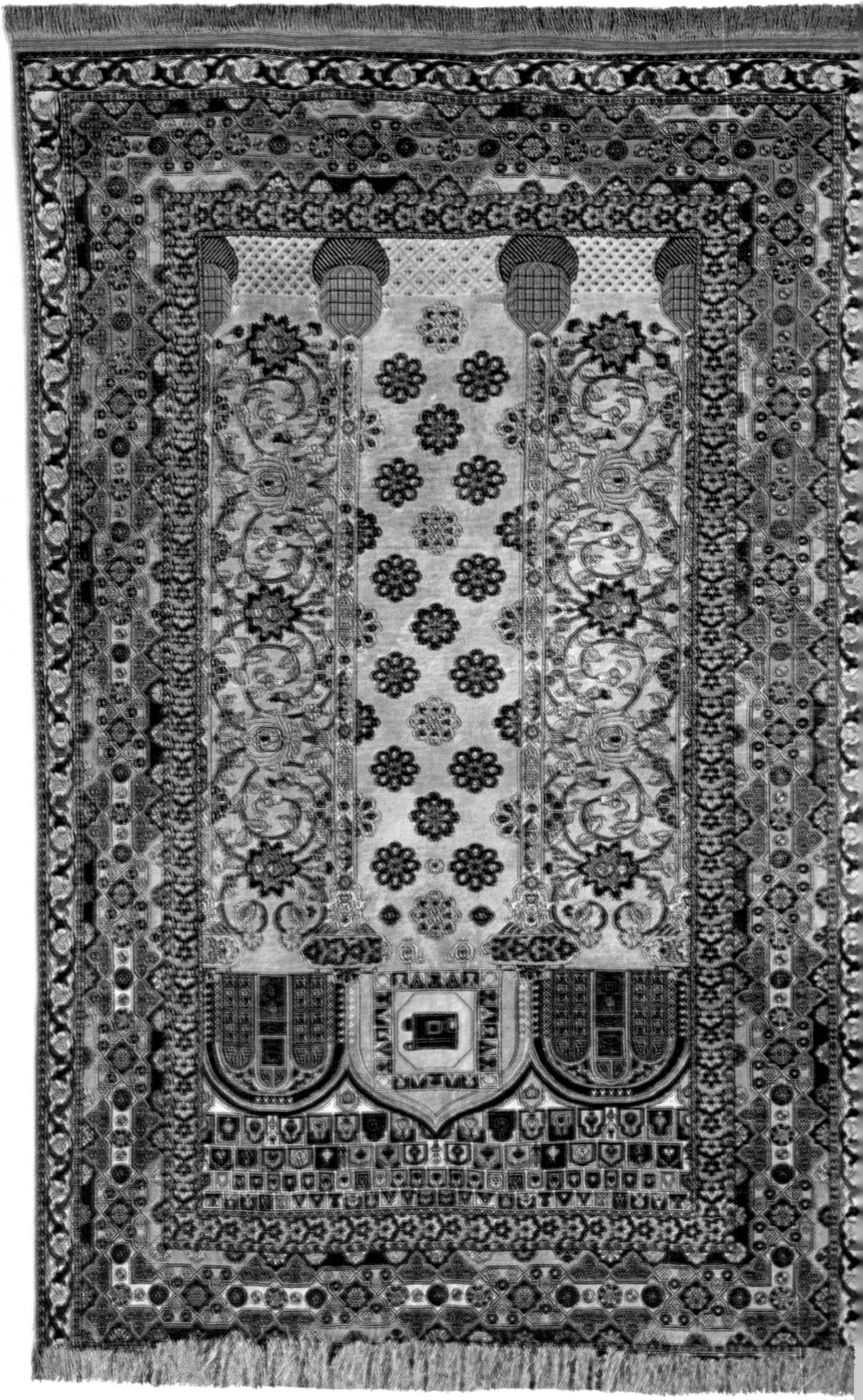

he Hazaras, Osbegs and Turkomans. Meshed, Khurasan, Turkbuff, Birjand, these carpets, made in the Khurasan district are alike, for they all have a purple-rose character. The main difference is that the Khurasan carpets have an all-over design, either in Herati or cone design and the Meshed, Turkbuff and Birjand carpets have medallions. Although, Birjand is 150 miles to the south, the rugs take on a similar look to the Mesheds. They have a Sehna knot, 90 to 400 per square inch.

Key

1. *Designs*	Fine.
2. *Knot*	Persian, or sometimes Turkish.
3. *Dyes*	Tend towards plum reds and dark greens.
4. *Wool*	Short and on average not always good quality.
5. *Side cords*	Overcast in wool.
6. *Ends (warp)*	Cotton.
7. *Weft*	Cotton.

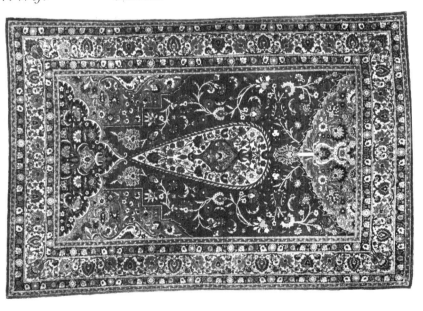

70. Meshed rug; 6 ft. 1 in. × 4 ft. 2 in. Unusual prayer niché with tree of life design, on a plum red ground.

MIR *(plate 71)*

Mir, from the Saraband district, have a short, lustrous pile and Sehna knot. They are strong and serviceable. They nearly

115

16. Koum Ka Pour rug. All silk. *Circa* 1900.

71. A fine Mir (Sarabend) rug; 6 ft. 2 in. × 3 ft. 10 in. Natural ground with small rose cones and trailing rose vine in border.

always have a repeating pattern of small cones, and a border-stripe with wavy stem-bearing cones. Runners are common.

Key

1. *Designs*	Plate shows a fine cone design, a typical example.
2. *Knot*	Persian.
3. *Dyes*	Madder red grounds with natural borders and blue cones.
4. *Wool*	Short and tough.

5. *Side cords*	Overcast in madder colours.
6. *Ends (warp)*	Cotton.
7. *Weft*	Cotton.

MOUSUL

Mousuls are woven by nomadic tribes on the western side of Persia, in the borders of Turkey and the outskirts of Hamadan. They are picturesque but vary enormously in design and are of poor quality.

Key

1. *Designs*	Copies of the Fereghans and Hamadans, but much coarser.
2. *Knot*	Turkish or Persian.
3. *Dyes*	Natural, blues and madders, sometimes pink grounds are seen.
4. *Wool*	Wool mixed with camel and goat hair, generally coarse.
5. *Side cords*	Overcast in wool.
6. *Ends (warp)*	Cotton.
7. *Weft*	Cotton.

72. Qum; 7 ft. × 4 ft. 6 in. *Circa* 1955.

117

Qum is a city situated between Kashan and Teheran, a large centre for modern weaving, where rugs are produced today in great quantities copying early hunting Persian miniature designs. The general colours used are natural, reddish terracottas, golds and blues. One can see today, floral carpets from the mausoleum of Shah Abbas II, at Qum, which are dated 1671.

Key

1. *Designs*	Not unlike the Ispahans.
2. *Knot*	Persian.
3. *Dyes*	Rust and blues.
4. *Wool*	Short and lustrous.
5. *Side cords*	Overcast wool or silk on silk rugs.
6. *Ends (warp)*	Cotton, or silk on silk rugs.
7. *Weft*	Cotton, or silk on silk rugs.

SAROUK *(plate 73)*

Sarouk is a city situated west of Kashan. They are fine, bold rugs with hard backs; and it is not unusual to find them with breaks and tears because of this hardness. The colours are usually strong, contrasts great. They are made with a Sehna knot and are usually very fine.

Key

1. *Designs*	Bold design.
2. *Knot*	Persian.
3. *Dyes*	Dark indigo, strong madder and green.
4. *Wool*	Like Kashan, short and lustrous.
5. *Side cords*	Overcast in wool.
6. *Ends (warp)*	Cotton.
7. *Weft*	Cotton.

SEHNA *(plate 74)*

Sehna is known as the 'City of the Persian knot'. These carpets are thin and have from 200 knots to the square in. There are no better carpets than these in the point of technique and delicacy of drawing. The average size of these is 8 ft. × 5½ ft. They have all-over patterns like cone diapers, floral and Herati.

Key

1. *Designs*	Fine and intricate.
2. *Knot*	Persian.
3. *Dyes*	Good madders, pale greens and soft yellows.
4. *Wool*	Very short and tough, a little dry (part silk pile rare).

73. Sarouk rug; 6 ft. 10 in. × 4 ft. 4 in. Indigo-blue ground, green central medallion with red corners. *Circa* 1850.

74. Sehna Kelim rug; 6 ft. 3 in. × 4 ft. 1 in. Pale yellow ground and border with a pale red medallion and corners, design mainly in green and rose.

5. *Side cords*	*Silk and mauve in colour.*
6. *Ends (warp)*	Cotton or silk.
7. *Weft*	Cotton or silk.

SHIRAZ *(Neriz, Faristan, Qashkai, Nifliz, Afshar) (plate 75)*
The capital of the province of Fars and the cradle of Persian
culture was the birth place of Persia's two great poets, Hafez
and Sa'di. Persepolis the city of the ancient world begun by

75. Quashkai rug; 8 ft. × 4 ft. 10 in. *Circa* 1950.

Darius the Great in 1521 B.C., only thirty miles from Shiraz,
was partially destroyed by Alexander in 323 B.C.; and today,
the soaring heights of its ravaged columns, winged colossi and
the other great sculptures, give solemn and majestic testimony

of its ancient glory. Nearby, in the sheer cliff-face of Naghshi-i-Rustam, are the four tombs of the Achemanian emporers, Darius the Great, Xerses, Artaxerxes and Darius II, hewn out of solid rock. Shiraz (Neriz, Faristan, Qashkai, Nifliz, Afshar), are names given to rugs made around Shiraz.

They are made with a Sehna knot and the very good wool gives a beautiful look to the rich colours. The cords are usually overcast with red and blue wool, also, sometimes tasseled. They resemble the Caucasian in designs and hexagonal medallions are very common. The finer rugs are called Mecca, Qashkai, etc., and the poorer types are classified as Afshar.

Key

1. *Designs*	Geometrical, in the main, but mixture of floral not unusual.
2. *Knot*	Persian.
3. *Dyes*	Tends towards dark rust, dark blue, although part floral designs have Kirman colours.
4. *Wool*	Short and lustrous.
5. *Side cords*	*Overcast in either two colours or bands of different colours.*
6. *Ends (warp)*	Usually a mixture of hair and wool (modern rugs have cotton).
7. *Weft*	*Red wool* or mixture of wool and hair *dyed red.* Modern rugs have white cotton.

TABRIZ (*plate 00*)

Tabriz is the second largest city of Iran and the first capital of the Il-Kanid Empire.

Tabriz carpets are made in and about the town of Tabriz in the north-west of Persia. They are considered to be one of the best type and most beautiful of Persian rugs. They have a Ghiordes knot, and from 200 knots to the square in. The pile is short and the texture is fine, the wool is hard and lustrous. They are known for their copies of famous sixteenth and seventeenth century hunting carpets, which were made in the nineteenth century under European influence. They are also renowned for their silk prayer rugs.

The plate shows a silk nineteenth-century medallion rug.

Key

1. *Designs*	Bold and elaborate. Silk prayer rugs.
2. *Knot*	Turkish (Ghiordes).
3. *Dyes*	Terracottas, blues and browns.
4. *Wool*	Hard, short pile.

76. Tabriz all silk pile rug; 5 ft. 6 in. × 4 ft. 3 in. *Circa* 1870.

5. *Side cords*	Double flat, see Type D, wool or silk.
6. *Ends (warp)*	Cotton, sometimes double (colour natural or terracotta) silk.
7. *Weft*	Cotton, silk, wool.

TEHERAN *(plate 77)*

A home for the famous crown jewels and the Peacock throne of Persia, kept in the vaulted rooms of the Central Bank, together with the 'Darya-i-Nur', the largest diamond of flawless lustre in the world, surrounded by a group of smaller diamonds, which dazzles the eye and staggers the imagination.

In 1962, the Marlik treasure of gold, bronze and ceramic was unearthed, whose origins date to 300 B.C. Teheran is the name given to fine modern carpets within the last seventy years, made on the outskirts of the capital city of Teheran. Sehna knot is used and the rugs are very fine and often mistaken for Ispahan.

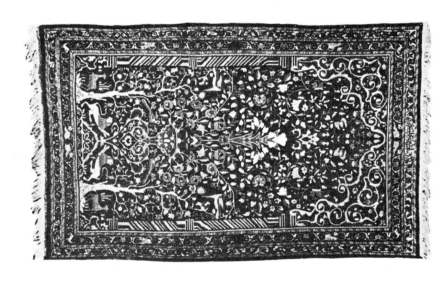

77. Teheran prayer rug; 6 ft. 4 in. × 4 ft. 6 in.

Key

| 1. *Designs* | See the illustration for a typical example. |
| 2. *Knot* | Persian. |

3. *Dyes*	Deep red, plum, deep blue and have very dark appearance.
4. *Wool*	Fine, short, lustrous wool.
5. *Side cords*	Single overcast, Type A of wool.
6. *Ends (warp)*	Cotton.
7. *Weft*	Cotton.

Y E Z D *(plate 78)*

Carpets made in the city of Yezd are often erroneously called Kirman, the designs are very similar, but their quality is usually far inferior.

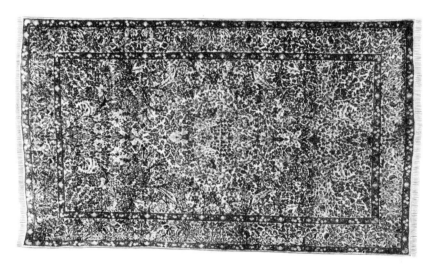

78. Yezd rug; 8 ft. × 4 ft. 9 in. *Circa* 1925.

Key

1. *Designs*	Similar to Kirman, but not so clear—see plate.
2. *Knot*	Persian.
3. *Dyes*	As Kirman.
4. *Wool*	Usually rather poor.
5. *Side cords*	Overcast in wool.
6. *Ends (warp)*	Cotton.
7. *Weft*	Cotton.

Zieglers, from the district of Sultanabad, look like large Fereghans and Bidjars, but of a much softer quality and texture. They were made for the European market from 1870.

Key

1. *Designs*   Large designs, semi-floral (stylised).
2. *Knot*   Turkish.
3. *Dyes*   Madder and dark blue with natural.
4. *Wool*   Long and lustrous.
5. *Side cords*   Overcast in wool.
6. *Ends (warp)* Cotton.
7. *Weft*   Cotton.

Poland

MASTER KEY TO POLAND

GENERAL:

Poland, 'nearly a country that never was'. In 1795 it was divided between Prussia, Austria and Russia, and it was not until 1918, that she was resurrected—then after twenty-one years (1939), she was again divided by Germany and Russia. Today, she is a communist state, with new frontiers, but she is still only three-quarters of her original size. With all her troubles, she still produced such famous people as, Marie Curie, Chopin, Paderewski, Michiewicz, (the poet), and Sienkiewicz, (author of Quo Vadis).

The experts differ regarding Polish carpets, some say carpets were never made in Poland, others say they were. Who is right? My view is that they both are, depending on which Polish carpet their views are based. For there are two types of Polish carpet: i. the Silk Polonaise; ii. the Woollen Polonaise.

At the museum in Lemberg, on the examination of old inventories, we find both types of carpets mentioned, the *Persian Polonaise* and the *Polish* carpets.

(*a*) *Polonaise silk*—we know that the Shah of Persia brought and presented to Duke Frederick of Holstein Gottop, six fine

79. Knotted pile Polish rug. Seventeenth century.

silk rugs in 1639 and that many more rugs and carpets followed of the same type.

(b) In the files of the Lemberg Museum, three carpets are mentioned, two of which are in the museum and are as follows: one with a coat of arms, dated 1698, and the second with a floral pattern. The third is the property of Professor Friederick Sarre.

In 1921, the Victoria and Albert Museum purchased a carpet, thinking it to be English, but soon after a carpet was seen in Paris, which differed only in pattern variation. This being so, both carpets were scrutinised very carefully, and found to be of the same origin—Polish. This carpet can be seen today in the Victoria and Albert Museum.

Other information is that, the Czartoryskis, (one of the richest Polish families) backed a workshop for making carpets, in Sluck, (now in the U.S.S.R.). Also, a Mr. Mazaraski in 1757 set up a workshop for weaving carpets in North-east Poland; Kowary was another centre for early carpets.

First compare the two illustrations, and then by using the key, you will find two entirely different carpets, one* *Persian Polonaise* (made in Persia), the other *Polish Polonaise* (made in Poland). *(See colour plate).

Key

1. *Designs*	(a) *Persian Polonaise*—as Persian fine and intricate;
	(b) *Polish Polonaise*—angular flowers almost English.
2. *Knot*	(a) *Persian Polonaise*—Persian knot;
	(b) *Polish Polonaise*—Turkish knot.
3. *Dyes*	(a) *Persian Polonaise*—all silk and have a good selection of vegetable dyes in a vast range of shades;
	(b) *Polish Polonaise*—pale greens, brown, natural and rose—few colours.
4. *Wool/silk*	(a) *Persian Polonaise*—good all silk pile;
	(b) *Polish Polonaise*—good all wool pile.
5. *Side cords*	(a) *Persian Polonaise*—very fine single silk;
	(b) *Polish Polonaise*—medium single wool.
6. *Ends (warp)*	(a) *Persian Polonaise*—all silk;
	(b) *Polish Polonaise*—all white wool.
7. *Weft*	(a) *Persian Polonaise*—silk and cotton;
	(b) *Polish Polonaise*—white wool.

Rumania

MASTER KEY TO RUMANIA

GENERAL:

Rumania was once the Roman province of Dacia under Emperor Trajan, who reigned from A.D. 98–117. Later it came under Turkish rule and it was not until 1878 that it became independent.

The main type of carpet weaving is the Kelim, a reversable tapestry, strong and hard-wearing beautiful designs. It is a folk art, and has no real beginning. There are no workshops, as such, it started in the homes as either blankets, then possibly wall coverings and eventually has become floor carpets: the Bessarabian Kelim.

There are three main areas of weaving:
  i. In the north, Moldavia, which is partly in Russia, and weavers keep designs rather intricate, the general texture is fine to very fine (weaving also in the town of Suceava).
  ii. In the south, Oltenian, similar rugs to the Moldavia, but with more primitive motifs, quality coarse to fine.
  iii. In the centre, amongst the Transylvannian mountains, the Hunedoare and Bamat, the designs are simple and geometrical, weave coarse to fine.

Modern rugs and carpets come from all these districts and many more besides—also hand-knotted pile carpets of any design, can be made-to-measure from the workshops, which have been installed since *1947*.

Key

1. *Designs*	See areas.
2. *Knot*	Kelims, reversable and tapestries; modern carpets have Persian knot.
3. *Dyes*	All Kelims of the nineteenth century and before have vegetable dyes, since early twentieth century aniline dyes have been used.
4. *Wool*	Wool on Kelims is first class, tough with a fine lustre; modern wool, as with all mill-spun yarn, is too soft and thin for hand-made rugs and carpets.
5. *Side cords*	Fine flat, and sometimes double cords, on modern carpets—one heavy overcast cords.

80. Rumanian Kelim from Moldavian district; 9 ft. 6 in. ×6 ft.

| 6. *Ends (warp)* | Until the nineteenth century, rugs were all wool, but during this period it was replaced by hemp or cotton (this fact is an important one for identification). |
| 7. *Weft* | This is the pile and makes up design, see wool. |

Russia

MASTER KEY TO RUSSIA

GENERAL:

Russia, Siberia, during 500 B.C. in the Pazyryk Valley in the Alti mountains (which border on south-western Mongolia and north-western China), a Prince of Alti died and was laid to rest in a burial mound. Sometime after, grave robbers broke in and took the metals and precious stones, but left a very fine hand-knotted rug, (why such a rug was not taken raises two points: i. was it too obvious an article to steal, or ii. was it so common and, therefore, not of much value). However, when they took flight, they left the burial chamber open—because of this, during some freak weather, which followed, the chamber filled with water and the water turned to ice, thus giving us a deep frozen rug.

In 1947–1949, S. J. Rudenko, the Russian archaeologist discovered these facts and the Alti rug can be seen today in the Hermitage Museum, Leningrad. Its size is 6 ft. × 6 ft. 6 in. (see illustration). The border design incorporates deer, warriors on horseback and horses with wings, the centre is made up of small panels, each containing a design of tail feathers and wings. This find is obviously the greatest of its kind in history, for it was hard to believe that anything was woven in 500 B.C., let alone the following facts:

(*a*) that rugs were made;

(*b*) that the use of fine hand-knotting in advance design, was known;

(*c*) that vegetable dyes were known and used in such a manner;

(*d*) that warrior horse rugs were used;

(*e*) that the composition of the design was so advanced, when one would expect something more primitive.

81. Russian carpet. *Circa* 1800.

The world has a lot to thank Mr. S. J. Rudenko for. From 500 B.C., we move to the earliest known town in the Ukraine—Kiev, founded in the ninth century A.D. Its religion was from Constantinople—a form of Christianity as practised by the Byzantine church—because of the religious attachment to Levant (Turkey), Russia drew its early art from the Middle East. Rugs and carpets were imported from Turkey, the Caucasus (Georgia) and Western Turkestan.

The most important period, as far as Russian carpets are concerned, is that of Catherine the Great (1762–1796), the Golden Age of Russia, when weaving took place in Kiev. The first carpets woven were for the palaces, which have Russian eagle designs in the corners, the real Zsars' carpets. Following these carpets, were the ones made for the forty families, which ruled Russia at that time (all land at that time belonged to either the Zsar or one of the forty families). Designs generally were a mass of intricate floral patterns, mostly on black grounds, and are the most striking of their type to be seen throughout the world.

BESSARABIA—part formerly in Rumania (Moldavia) and the Ukraine. Moldavia is an area, which many centuries prior, was weaving floral type, folk weave Kelims (Ghilims). In the eighteenth century, under the supervision of the Russian court, the finest Kelims evolved, in designs similar to the Ukraine (Kiev) carpets (mass floral pattern).

In the nineteenth century, Russia was first unsuccessfully invaded by Napoleon (1812), then the Crimean War (1854–1856), then the Freeing of the Serfs in 1861 (which gave ten million land workers freedom) and who were also helped to buy their land. Gradually, the country became weaker. In 1878, Russia annexed the Caucasus. In 1904–5, there was the Russo-Japanese war, in which Russia was thoroughly beaten, and in 1917 the Revolution. The important points relating to these events were:

(a) that after the Crimean war, very few carpets were produced in Kiev;

(b) the annexation of the Caucasus 1878, meant that all Caucasian rugs had to be traded through Russia proper;

(c) that with the Revolution (1917) came the anexation of Western Turkestan, which meant that all Bokharas had to be traded through Russia, (hence the name Russian Bokhara).

Some tribes objected to the setting up of a Trading Company, with whom they were forced to trade, so they crossed over the border and started weaving around Meshed in Persia, (hence the name Persian Bokhara). Today, we import from Russia, the Bokhara and Caucasian only; the Ukrainian carpets, unfortunately, have ceased to be produced.

Key

1. *Designs*	Apart from the Alti rug and the special Zsar carpets, they were a mass of floral patterns, the later carpets had vases of flowers in central positions.
2. *Knot*	Turkish in the carpets; Bessarabian were of tapestry weave (reversable).
3. *Dyes*	Black grounds, which made them colourful,

133

	although never as bright as the Spanish or French carpets.
4. *Wool*	Good quality in carpets and Kelims.
5. *Side cords*	Fine flat cords on carpets and Kelims.
6. *Ends (warp)*	Wool, or wool and hair on carpets and Kelims.
7. *Weft*	Wool, or wool and hair on carpets; pile of Kelims were of all wool and made up the design.

Spain

MASTER KEY TO SPAIN

GENERAL:

The history of Spain dates back to 1100 B.C., when the city of Cadiz was founded by the Phoenicians. The history of the carpets started early but there is no evidence until the eleventh century A.D. (the El Cid period). Fragments have now been discovered of the eleventh and early twelfth century, which clarify this.

In the thirteenth century, there were firstly the Quedlingburg carpets, *circa* 1200, and secondly that in 1225, when Eleanor of Castile was brought to England by Edward I, Spanish rugs were hung from the windows to mark the event.

In the fourteenth century, records show that a quantity of carpets were received by Egypt from Spanish Morocco, and that fourteen cities were weaving carpets in Spain.

In the fifteenth century, there were three carpets, of which two were found in the nineteenth century in the convent of Sa. Clara, Valencia. These two were made for the Enriquez family which held the position of Admiral of Castile; both have coats of arms, and the first dates back to 1405, the second 1473. The third carpet, if found, has not been recognised as such, as its only record is that Queen Isabela of Castile sent a letter of many thanks to the people of the city of Castile, for the carpet she received from them.

1492, was an important year in the history of Spain, firstly the last stronghold of the Moors fell (Granada) after 700 years of rule, and secondly it was the year Columbus sailed for the New World, an interesting point being, that he was the son of a weaver from Genoa.

82. Spanish sixteenth century rug.

By the sixteenth century, Spanish art was at its zenith. Painters such as Velasquez, Luis de Vargas, Luis de Morales and the famous Greek painter, Domenico Theotacopouli (nicknamed 'El Greco') showed rugs on floors and tables in their paintings, but they seemed to be of Turkish origin by design.

During the seventeenth, eighteenth and nineteenth centuries, many rugs and carpets were made and good examples are to be seen in textile museums all over the world. Late nineteenth and twentieth century carpets have two styles, firstly they copied the old designs and method of weaving, secondly they make a Spanish Savonnerie, which can be bought today, both made by hand and of excellent value.

SPANISH AUBUSSONS were made in the nineteenth century and are virtually the same as the French except that the colours are much stronger and bolder—black is used to highlight the designs and a very bright, blood red, these two colours make them very easily identifiable.

The following chart shows the make-up of known carpets, from the early periods to the present day:

Century	*Towns*	*Weft*	*Warp*	*Pile*
12th	Letur—Alcarez	Goat	Goat	Wool
14/15th	Letur—Alcaraz	Goat	Goat	Wool
15th	Letur—Cuenca—Alcaraz	Wool	Goat	Wool
16th	Alcaraz	Wool	Goat	Wool
16th	Cuenca	Goat	Goat	Goat
17th	Not known exactly, as many centres	Wool	Wool	Wool
18th	Not known exactly, as many centres	Linen	Linen	Wool
18th	Not known exactly, as many centres	Wool	Wool	Wool
19th	Alpujarra	Linen	Linen	Wool
20th	Many centres	Jute	Wool	Wool
20th	Savonneries, many centres	Wool	Cotton	Wool

Key

1. *Designs*   Bold and almost crude but with simplicity of true art.
2. *Knot*   Spanish knot, see *Knot* diagram—Spanish

	carpets are very easy to identify because of these knots.
3. *Dyes*	Bold, strong colours, even the early carpets of yellow and blue only are strong, later carpets their blues, reds and blacks are almost violent.
4. *Wool*	Good wool, but can be a little dry, see chart.
5. *Side cords*	Early carpets have more of a selvage edge than a proper cord, almost like canvas. Some have light overcast cords, twentieth century carpets have modern overcast cords.
6. *Ends (warp)*	See chart. Aubussons have Spanish linen or cotton.
7. *Weft*	See chart. In Aubussons the weft is the pile, as it is tapestry weave, and is made of all wool.

Sweden

MASTER KEY TO SWEDEN

GENERAL:

Sweden, the home of the Goths and Vikings, some of which foraged and traded across Russia, sailing down its rivers to Byzantium (Istanbul), where they formed a part of Emperor Varingian's guard. This point is important, because, the work of Swedish carpets is akin to the Ukranian rugs of Moldavia, which possibly means that on their return examples of work must have been taken to Sweden and copied. For as long ago as the fifteenth century, a type of tapestry Kelim carpet was woven in the then thirteen provinces of Sweden. The most important of these provinces are as follows: Torna, Bara, Skytts, Wennenhog, Harjagers and Oxie. Their designs are shown in the two illustrations, firstly one from the Oxie district, and secondly a twentieth century rug made in 1930. The styles remained unchanged from the fifteenth century, one can in fact buy these types of rugs today, from the handicraft industry in Sweden.

Key

1. *Designs*	Two main types, geometrical and semi-floral, (see illustrations).

83. Swedish rug. *Circa* 1930.

138

2. *Knot*	Tapestry weave.
3. *Dyes*	Vegetable dyes up to the twentieth century.
4. *Wool*	Good quality, tough wool.
5. *Side cords*	With tapestry work, they have attached fine tapestry Kelim of five to seven strands.
6. *Ends (warp)*	Wool or linen is used.
7. *Weft*	Wool, as weft is design and pile.

Turkestan

GENERAL:

A country of tribesmen, who wander from the Black Sea to China, moving with the seasons to better pastures for their flocks, across the grassy steppes, but always returning to the same known tribal ground once a year to make claim, and woe-betide anyone who dare settle there.

During their travels, rugs and small carpets are made and periodically they are brought into Bokhara, which is the main selling and bartering market for carpets. The rugs all look about the same, and no-one took the trouble to find out any more about them, in fact, everyone assumed they were all made in or around Bokhara. Eventually, when the true facts came to light, it was impossible to change the names, and even today, rather than confuse clients, dealers call them all Bokharas and if the client seems interested, they explain from which tribe.

MASTER KEY TO TURKESTAN

Turkestan, Turkoman and Bokhara are all one and must not be confused with the Turkey carpet. Turkestan is the country, Turkoman the rugs woven in that country, and Bokhara a name given in the broadest sense to the types of tribal rugs produced.

The tribes are as follows:
1. *Tekké*—Bokhara.
2. *Yomud*—Bokhara.
3. *Pinde* (Punjeh)—Bokhara.
4. *Chaudor*—Bokhara.

84. Turkestan Salor saddle bag rug.

5. *Salor*—Bokhara.
6. *Saryk*—Bokhara.

The prayer rugs are called Hatchlie (Khatchlie), so a Tekké prayer rug would be a 'Tekké Hatchlie Bokhara' to be exact.

Other types which I have separated are the Ersaris and Beshir; apart from these two tribes, which will be dealt with later, the others have almost the same design throughout, with the exception of the type and shape of the Guls (medallions) or octagonals which repeat throughout the field, and in some cases the ground colour. The Hatchlie, or prayer rug, consists of a type of large cross (believed to have developed unknowingly after the crusades, hence the cross on a Mohammaden rug). The four quarters of the design consist of many small candle holders. The top of the cross has a niché (in some rugs, there are as many as nine small nichés). The borders and ends differ only slightly with each tribe. The diagrams (see appendix) will help you to identify the Guls of each tribe.

ERSARI rugs would be best recognised by their outstanding designs, which are either a trellis work with guls or diamond pattern in each section, or else a zig-zag design. The general colouring is medium madder red ground, blue-green and a great deal of yellow is used.

140

BESHIRS are from the district east of Khiva. They are of coarse and medium texture, and the patterns are more floral than those of other central Asian rugs. The chief colours are red, brown, dark blue with an abundance of yellow. Prayer rugs are rare. See plate for a typical example.

Key

1. *Designs* — These are tribal and can be identified by the Guls (medallions octagonal in shape) or other features mentioned, (see diagrams).

2. *Knot* — Mostly Persian (Sehna), but Turkish (Ghiordes) are not uncommon.

3. *Dyes* — Ground colours are as follows:
   1. *Tekké*—Rose (madder red).
   2. *Yomud*—Brown-red.
   3. *Pinde*—Brown-red.
   4. *Chaudor*—Plum-red to brown.
   5. *Salor*—Deep mauve-brown.
   6. *Saryk*—Brown-red.

4. *Wool* *(silk)* *(cotton)* — The Turkoman tribes, with the exception of the Beshirs, all have hard, tough resilient wool, and it is difficult to make a thumb impression on the pile (the wool of the Pakistan Bokharas copies can too easily be parted), which is a good test. The Beshir wool is not as tough, although it seems to have a better lustre. Another point is that Beshirs are hardly ever fine. Small parts of the Bokhara design may contain silk pile and cotton pile, but rugs containing either are rare (cotton is natural and the silk is green, yellow or cyclamen).

   During the last twenty years all silk pile Bokharas have been woven and, in most cases, are difficult to surpass in quality and design.

   Merserised cotton Bokhara design rugs have been produced in Turkey, which look like silk and which have fooled many people who thought they had found the bargain of the year.

5. *Side cords* — Single wool overcast on most Bokharas *coloured blue*. Ersaris are single or double overcast in ground colours. Beshirs are double flat wool or check pattern with blue, (see cord diagrams).

6. *Ends (warp)*   Goat hair and wool; camel hair and wool, *cotton is never used* (one of the best points of recognition).

7. *Weft*   As for Ends (warp).

85. Turkestan—Hatchlie Pinde Turkoman rug (Bokhara); 5 ft. 4 in. × 4 ft. 6 in. An unusual prayer rug woven with wool, cotton and silk. *Circa* 1810.

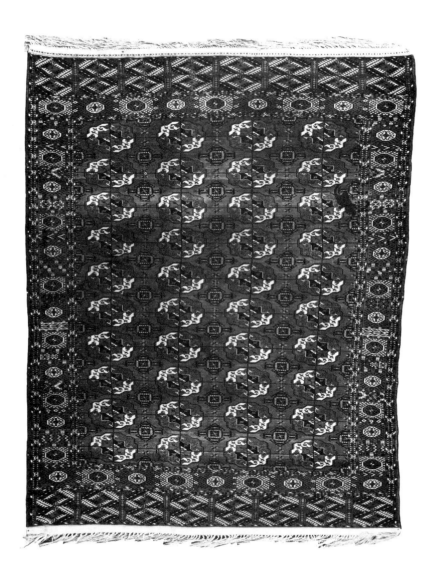

86. A fine Tekke Bokhara rug. Rose ground; 5 ft. 10 in. × 4 ft. 6 in.

Turkestan-Eastern

MASTER KEY TO EASTERN TURKESTAN

GENERAL:

Today, Eastern Turkestan is partly in the Chinese Republic and partly in the Soviet Socialist Republic. It has a population of approximately three million, who live in just over one million square miles. There are twelve main cities, some of which are very small. The northern part borders on Mongolia and Russia, where the famous Alti rug was found, dating back to 500 B.C. (see *Russia*—general).

The population is made up of Eastern Turks, Chinese, Mongols and the Kazak tribes. Today, archaeologists are still finding ruins dating back 2,000 years.

All the carpets from this vast area were brought into Samarkand, and sold or bartered. For many years, these have been classified as such, even today the word 'Samarkand' appeals to dealers and customers alike and, therefore, the use of Kashgar, Khotan, Yarkand and Kansu (Kansu is in China) is only employed by the connoisseur to distinguish the various pieces. However, if you are very interested in these rugs, I can advise you to purchase the book by Hans Bidder—'Carpets from Eastern Turkestan'.

Key

1. *Designs*	The designs seem to be struggling away from the Chinese influence and yet not Persian, (see illustration).
2. *Knot*	Persian.
3. *Dyes*	Mostly vegetable, although this century has brought a little aniline, possibly no more because of the remoteness of the country.
4. *Wool*	Usually very good, but bad examples still appear.
5. *Side cords*	Simple, single cords of wool, sometimes cotton is used.
6. *Ends (warp)*	Cotton.
7. *Weft*	Cotton.

144

87. Eastern Turkestan—Khotan rug; 8 ft. 10 in. × 4 ft. 9 in. On a pale yellow ground with aubergine medallion and borders. *Circa* 1880.

88. Eastern Turkestan
Yarkand runner. *Circa* 1800.

146

Turkey

GENERAL :

The history of Asia Minor clearly dates back to the fifth century B.C., so it is difficult to believe that the earliest examples of Turkish carpets of the fouteenth century, were the first woven.

The obvious answer lies in the fact that Turkey became the battle ground of nations, who wanted the 'gateway' to the Far East.

In the early sixteenth century, under Solyman the Magnificent (the Grand Turk), Turkey became the most powerful country of the Middle East, ruling fifty million people from the Black Sea, around the Mediterranean to Morocco. In these years an abundance of carpets were produced and can be seen in museums all over the world. Their designs like the Ottoman architecture were bold and elegant. It was during this period, that the English Cardinal Wolsey negotiated sixty Turkey carpets from Venice—described as Turkey *Damascene* carpets. I would like to clarify the use or mis-use of the word 'Damascene'. It was in fact used to describe the design and *not* the place it was made in (Damascus), as by the sixteenth century, Damascene work was known not only throughout the Middle and Far East, but also most parts of Europe (Damascene being the art of inlaying gold, silver or copper wire onto the surface of steel or bronze).

Today, Turkish carpets are not that well-known for their masterpieces, in fact.

MASTER KEY TO TURKEY

When you hear the words 'Turkey Carpet', the first thing that comes to mind is an old-fashioned red and blue thick pile carpet with an enormous design. This is because thousands of Turkey carpets were produced and sent all over the world, and owing to their size and outstanding colour, they became an household word. Carpets such as the Borlu, Ghiordes, Sparta, and Sivas were the carpets produced before and since the Turkey, but as their designs were subdued, most laymen classified them as Persian. The old Turkish carpet was the world's finest carpet, and, at its peak, second to none (see colour plate).

Turkish rugs not only have a look of their own, but they are also very pliable, much more so than any other Oriental rug. They use cotton, merserised cotton (which looks like silk) and rayon pile. The only rugs, which could be confused with Turkish today are the modern Belouchestan (Pakistan), but as they have a Persian knot, they are easily defined.

Out of the eighteen classifications which I have listed, the ones which you will most likely see are the ones made since 1860. These are: Melas, Bergama, Turkeys, Sparta, Sivas, Hereké and a small quantity of others which are more difficult to define and which come from small centres all over Turkey. Once again a local antique rug dealer will be able to guide you. The other ten listed are either twelfth to eighteenth century, and you are most likely to see these in museums.

Key

1. *Designs*	As you study the plates you will notice a definite style of motif which is unlike the Persian or any other country for that matter. The only type which could be confused is the Sivas and Hereké. Many hunting and animal prayer rugs produced, all thin and pliable.
2. *Knot*	All have Turkish knot, so this is therefore a most important means of identification (not to be confused with the few Persian towns using a Turkish knot).
3. *Dyes*	Most modern carpets have a bluish appearance, see individual classification.
4. *Wool*	Heavy texture in carpets, except for Anatolians, Herekés and Sivas. Rugs have medium texture, cotton is used in the pile by many weavers, in order to highlight designs.
5. *Side cords*	All have double, flat side cords of wool or cotton—a quick way to identify a Turkish rug. (*N.B.*—Tabriz and Heriz are the only towns using double flat cords in Persia.)
6. *Ends (warp)*	The old rugs (twelfth to nineteenth century) had woollen wefts and warps, except Mudjur rugs. In the last ninety years weavers have used cotton, even fakers made the mistake of using cotton instead of wool—which is a good point to watch for when buying so-called 200 years old Turkish rugs.

7. Weft   The same applicable as in Ends (warp). Bergama make a feature of their 'Kelim ends', by weaving small designs of triangles usually in a central position.

89. Silk Anatolian; 5 ft. 7 in. × 4 ft. 2 in. *Circa* 1910.

90. Anatolian Pandama rug; 5 ft. 9 in. × 3 ft. 10 in. Blue-black ground with an all-over grey-green effect.

ANATOLIAN *(plate 90)*

Anatolian carpets are from the Anatolian plateau. They are soft and pliable, with a lustrous pile. The chief colours are red, yellow, blue, fawn and shades of brown. Ghiordes knot. Woollen rugs have approximately 45 to 150 knots per square in. ; silk rugs anything up to 300 knots per square in. Anatolian rugs, woven in the nineteenth and early twentieth centuries, of wool and cotton pile, tend to be finer than the average.

Key

1. *Designs*	Copies of sixteenth and seventeenth century rugs in pleasing designs.
2. *Knot*	Turkish.
3. *Dyes*	Soft colours, except for indigo. Slate blue and grey used extensively.

150

4. *Wool*   Short and lustrous.
5. *Side cords*   Double flat cord.
6. *Ends (warp)*   Cotton.
7. *Weft*   Cotton.

BERGAMA *(plate 91)*; colour plate 9

Bergama (from the ancient Pergamun). The colours are rich and dark, geometrical in design with large and small-type medallions. Ghiordes knot, approximately 50 to 80 knots per square in. Often mistaken for Kazak.

Key

1. *Designs*   Geometrical, often mistaken for Kazaks, (see plates).
2. *Knot*   Turkish.
3. *Dyes*   Madder, dark blues and a little yellow.
4. *Wool*   Short, heavy and lustrous.
5. *Side cords*   Double flat, woollen blue cord.
6. *Ends (warp)* Cotton or wool and hair, (antique pieces in wool).
7. *Weft*   Cotton or wool and hair, (antique pieces in wool). Kelim ends—diagonal motif in central position on most rugs.

91. Bergama rug; 4 ft. 6 in. × 4 ft. 2 in. *Circa* 1850.

151

Known as the Turkey with the pastel look, is sometimes very finely woven. Nearly all the designs were made to order and colours are so pastel they are delightful with French gilt furniture, and are called on many occasions the poor man's Savonnerie.

Key

1. *Designs*   Never geometrical—copies of famous Persian designs.
2. *Knot*   Turkish.
3. *Dyes*   Some of the pastel shades have since faded to natural.
4. *Wool*   Good quality with lustre.
5. *Side cords*   Double flat.
6. *Ends (warp)*   Cotton.
7. *Weft*   Cotton.

92. Ghiordes rug; 6 ft. 5 in. × 4 ft. 2 in. *Circa* 1750.

GHIORDES *(plate 92)*

Ghiordes'—the city of the Turkish knot—are the most prized Turkish carpets. They are fairly finely woven, and the pile is so short that the wool never looks very lustrous. The principal colours are red, blue and white. The plain ground of the niché is usually blue, red, natural or green. In the later specimens the red inclines towards crimson. In some pieces there is an added silk fringe at the corners. The arch is usually supported by two columns; 65 to 110 knots per square in.

The modern Ghiordes carpet is rather coarse and could be classified as a type of fine pastel ground Turkey with a Persian type design.

Key

1. *Designs*	All over design carpets, prayer rug designs, and double-ended prayer rug designs, called Kiz Ghiordes.
2. *Knot*	Turkish.
3. *Dyes*	Good red, yellows and blues, and pale green.
4. *Wool*	Short, tough pile.
5. *Side cords*	Double flat wool.
6. *Ends (warp)*	Wool.
7. *Weft*	Wool, dyed red on Basra Ghiordes.

HEREKE SILKS *(and wool) (front cover)*

Hereke silks and wool carpets and rugs are made in the factory of the Sultan at Hereke. With Persian patterns, they have many colours and some contain silver and gold metallic thread. They have as many as 800 knots to the square in.

Key

1. *Designs*	Fine, intricate designs beautifully drawn; many animal and hunting designs.
2. *Knot*	Turkish.
3. *Dyes*	Pastel colours.
4. *Wool*	Silk of the finest quality—short pile.
5. *Side cords*	Double flat cords in silk on silk rugs and in wool on woollen rugs.
6. *Ends (warp)*	Silk on silk rugs, wool and cotton.
7. *Weft*	Silk on silk rugs, wool and cotton.

KELIMS; colour plate 1

Kelims (Shahquord, Gigim) are the two categories, Shahquord being reversable and Gigim woven in tapestry style with loose ends at the back, generally worked in quaint, bright geometrical designs.

Key
1. *Designs*   Stylised, semi-geometrical.
2. *Knot*   Tapestry weave and reversable.
3. *Dyes*   Dark reds, gay colours.
4. *Wool*   Good quality.
5. *Side cords*   Tapestry cords.
6. *Ends (warp)* Cotton, wool, or goats hair.
7. *Weft*   Is the pile and is made of wool.

KOULA *(Kourmur Jur Koula) (plate 93)*
Koula is a rug very similar to Ghiordes, but usually coarser in texture. The colours are mostly yellow and blue. The centres are usually with motifs of cypress trees, or stylised flowers. The borders often consist of a large number of narrow stripes, each filled with small detached blossoms or buds, sometimes called fly-borders. Ghiordes knot, 65 to 110 per square in.

A Kourmur Jur Koula is a double-ended prayer rug.

Key
1. *Designs*   General appearance of Koula—yellow and blue Kourmur Jur—brick red and yellow border.
2. *Knot*   Turkish.
3. *Dyes*   Yellow, blue and brown.
4. *Wool*   Good quality, short pile.
5. *Side cords*   Double flat wool.
6. *Ends (warp)* Wool.
7. *Weft*   Wool.

KOUM KA POUR *(silks) (plate 00)*
Koum Ka Pour made in the suburbs of Istanbul, the name meaning, 'Gates to the Sands', where the factory for weaving very fine rugs was situated. The master weaver, was a man named Kanata, who produced the finest rugs in the world, made of silk and metallic gold and silver thread. These were made under the patronage of the Sultan of Turkey. There were approximately 1,000 knots per square in. Kanata was one of the only weavers who was able to make metallic rose petals of different colours embossed in the borders and in centre panels, using as many as eight or nine colours. Woven from 1890 to 1910.

Key
1. *Designs*   The finest ever produced in the world.
2. *Knot*   Turkish.
3. *Dyes*   Subtle, pastel colours.

93. Kourmur Jur Koula; 6 ft. 2 in. ×4 ft. Double-ended prayer rug.

4. *Wool*	Only made in silk, short 'cut well'.
5. *Side cords*	Fine flat silk cords, double or treble.
6. *Ends (warp)*	Silk.
7. *Weft*	Silk.

LADIK *(plate 94)*

Ladik (named from Laodicea) are erroneously known as Ghiordes rugs. The colours are chiefly red and blue. Although, mostly bright, sometimes a rich, quieter colour effect is found. There is a wide cross-panel, containing tall upright tulips, above or below the niché. Ghiordes knot, 65 to 110 knots per square in. (See plate.)

94. Seventeenth century Ladik rug; 6 ft. × 3 ft. 4 in. Madder-red ground with blue niché and tulip field with a saffron-yellow border.

Key

1. *Designs*	Prayer rug, one part niché the other part tulips, very easily distinguished by this.
2. *Knot*	Turkish.
3. *Dyes*	Red centre, with yellow, pale blue or red section holding tulips.
4. *Wool*	Medium texture, short pile.
5. *Side cords*	Double flat wool.
6. *Ends (warp)*	Wool.
7. *Weft*	Wool, sometimes dyed red.

Known as Rhodian, is of a coarse texture with a semi-geometrical design. The rug has two prayer arches side by side with a thin dividing column. Woven on a blue ground with yellow, natural and orange borders.

Key

1. *Designs*	Double prayers with geometrical motifs above arch, (see plate).
2. *Knot*	Turkish.
3. *Dyes*	Blue with orange, brown and a little red.
4. *Wool*	Good but of coarse texture.
5. *Side cords*	Double flat wool.
6. *Ends (warp)*	Wool.
7. *Weft*	Wool.

95. Makri rug (Rhodes); 6 ft. 6 in. ×4 ft. 3 in. *Circa* 1800. Note double prayer.

MELAS *(plate 96)*

Melas (named from Melassa) are soft and pliable carpets, with a fairly short and lustrous pile. The leading colour is rust red, but there is often a good deal of yellow in the border. Antiques have a quality of mauve, light blue or pastel green in the

96. Turkish Antique Melas; 5 ft. 8 in. × 4 ft.

semi-geometrical design. The top of the prayer niché usually forms a diamond-shape. Sixty to 80 knots per square in.

Key

1. *Designs*   Noted for their niché and unusual borders.

2. *Knot*	Turkish.
3. *Dyes*	Rust red, pale yellow almost washed out, pale green and slate blue.
4. *Wool*	Short and tough.
5. *Side cords*	Double flat wool.
6. *Ends (warp)*	Wool.
7. *Weft*	Wool.

MUDJUR *(plate 97)*

Mudjur situated in the middle of Turkey produced attractive red ground prayer rugs with unusual borders, which are easily recognisable. They are generally coarse in texture.

97. Mudjur rug; 5 ft. 6 in. × 4 ft. *Circa* 1850.

Key

1. *Designs*	Made in prayer rugs, are rare runners.
2. *Knot*	Turkish.
3. *Dyes*	Red centre door (niché) with subdued borders.
4. *Wool*	Coarse texture and short pile.
5. *Side cords*	Double flat cord in cotton.
6. *Ends (warp)*	Cotton or wool.
7. *Weft*	Cotton or wool.

98. Anatolian saph;
10 ft. × 3 ft. 2 in.

Family prayer rug, each male having his own niché (door prayer), made in the last forty years in great quantities.

Key

1. *Designs*	A runner-type with prayer arches across its width like a row of bottles on a shelf; the arches or doors are in plain colours and the remainder of the runner is the same as usual with its normal border.
2. *Knot*	Turkish.
3. *Dyes*	Good wool and good silks.
4. *Wool*	Made in wool, silk or merserised cotton pile.
5. *Side cords*	Double stranded.
6. *Ends (warp)*	Cotton or silk (some silk pile rugs have cotton base).
7. *Weft*	Cotton or silk (some silk pile rugs have cotton base).

SIVAS *(plate 99)*

Sivas, from the city of Sivas, are often mistaken for Persian. They are extremely finely woven. The main way to distinguish from the Persian is to note the colours. The red has a blue-mauve appearance, the pink has a blue tinge, and the blue has a slate look; the wool is very lustrous and medium in length. Although fine, a Sivas rarely seems to have the clarity of a similar quality Persian. From 110 to 300 knots per square in.

99. Sivas; 14 ft. 10 in. × 11 ft. 5 in.

1. *Designs*   Fine designs with medallion centres, (see plate for average design).
2. *Knot*   Turkish.
3. *Dyes*   Bluish-pinks, dark blues.
4. *Wool*   Short rather tough with lustre.
5. *Side cords* Fine double cord.
6. *Ends (warp)* Cotton.
7. *Weft*   Cotton.

SPARTA *(plate 100)*

Sparta, from the city of Isparta, is similar to the Sivas but much coarser. Colours and textures are the same although the cities are some 600 miles apart. From 50 to 120 knots per square in.

100. Sparta; 23 ft. 10 in. × 12 ft. 1 in.

Key

1. *Designs*   Copies most designs, but always coarser.
2. *Knot*   Turkish.
3. *Dyes*   Bluish-pinks, slate blues and bluish-greens.
4. *Wool*   Heavy and coarse.
5. *Side cords* Heavy double cord.
6. *Ends (warp)* Cotton.
7. *Weft*   Cotton.

Originating from Asia Minor, probably Ushak, these rugs were sent through Transylvania, who taxed them and from whence the name derived. The colouring of the earlier rugs was subdued. The eighteenth century pieces are more Persian than

101. Transylvanian rug. Eighteenth century. Note the geometrical cartouches in border.

Turkish in the method of the central field and spandrels. However, they have the skeleton geometrical design, cartouché border, coarse weaving and Ghiordes knot.

Key

1. *Designs*   Easy to distinguish by their borders, which have geometrical cartouchés.
2. *Knot*   Turkish.
3. *Dyes*   Reds and blues.
4. *Wool*   Medium to coarse texture—short pile.
5. *Side cords* Double flat wool.
6. *Ends (warp)* Wool.
7. *Weft*   Wool.

USHAK *(Konia, Holbein) (plate 102)*

Ushak (Konia, Holbein) carpets date from the fifteenth century, and are woven with a Ghiordes knot. The earliest have large circular medallions and Turkish scroll designs. The pile is of wool, with occasionally a little white cotton. The texture is rather coarse. The colours are red, dark blue, yellow, white, black, light blue, green, green-blue and purple—these have been placed in preference of use—and an average of seven colours is usual. Holbein, made in Ushak, is so-called after the Flemish painter, Holbein, who used this type of rug in paintings. Konias were not woven until the late sixteenth century. Sixteen to 170 knots per square in.

Key

1. *Designs*   Large designs, on average Konias are more geometrical.
2. *Knot*   Turkish.
3. *Dyes*   Dark reds, dark blues.
4. *Wool*   Medium to coarse texture.
5. *Side cords* Double flat wool.
6. *Ends (warp)* Wool.
7. *Weft*   Wool.

YURUK

Yuruk, these carpets are sometimes erroneously called Kazak or Derbend. They have from 50 to 170 knots per square in. They have a long, soft and lustrous pile. They are made by the Kurdish mountaineers of Eastern Turkey, and should be distinguished by the colours: brown, rust, red, blue and a little white. The general appearance is dark. They also have heavy fringes of goat hair and wool.

102. Ushak sixteenth century; 13 ft. 5 in. × 7 ft. 5 in.

Key

1. *Designs*	Geometrical.
2. *Knot*	Turkish.
3. *Dyes*	All very dark and crude.
4. *Wool*	Coarse.
5. *Side cords*	Double flat wool.
6. *Ends (warp)*	Cotton or mixture of goat hair and wool.
7. *Weft*	Cotton or mixture of goat hair and wool.

Renovations

'A stitch in time saves nine', is certainly an understatement where valuable textiles are concerned. If they are not properly cared for in good time, they may gradually deteriorate beyond repair and become a total and irreparable loss. And the preservation of these beautiful things is not only a matter of their value in the present, or near future, but also a duty to posterity.

The future prospects of the ancient weaving craft, inspired in the past by religious or venerable sentiments are rather dim. Indeed, this art is becoming practically extinct even in the Orient. Therefore, if we fail to preserve what we are fortunate to have inherited from past generations all we shall leave to posterity will be machine made replicas or prints of ancient designs, and a few specimens preserved in various museums. The modern article, mass-produced as quickly and cheaply as possible, cannot be expected to outlive its owners, which perhaps is the kindest thing that can be said about it.

The cleaning and repair of carpets requires great care and skill. The value of an antique carpet will rise or fall according to the quality of repair. For one thing, a poor repair from unseasoned modern wools will be painfully apparent in a year, through the fading of colours, while a repair made with wools carefully boiled and matched may well last for at least a dozen years before fading shows. If you possess any antique rugs or carpets, you will be well advised to send them for cleaning or repair to experts.

In the first place they require to be cleaned and, if necessary, overhauled once a year, the cost of repairs being comparatively small if undertaken in good time. Domestic vacuum cleaners, especially if they sweep and beat at the same time, are very useful and should be applied regularly, but it must be remembered that they do not guarantee to remove more than 70 per cent of the dust and grit which embeds itself deeper into the pile. The proper process of wet cleaning after beating will dissolve and extract the remaining dirt and give the carpet a new lease of life. Sand and grit act as knives on the pile when trodden upon, especially when the wool is allowed to become dry and brittle, and will also make the carpet more appetising for moths. In short, renovation is preservation.

A tip to keep your rugs free of grit is to place them face (pile) down on a hard floor and vacuum the back, the vibration will certainly push the grit to the floor. This should be done every three to six months.

Observation Test

I would not like to remember how many homes I have visited where I have pointed out different motifs on rugs and tapestries, which the owners had never seen—although they have had them in their possession many years, sometimes a lifetime. What a pity most peoples' observations are very poor. So at this stage I believe it is very important to improve your ability to observe. I have set you below, a few tests, I am sure you will find them interesting.

1. OBSERVATION
Take a note pad and pencil and write the name of your closest friend in the top of the sheet, by memory write down the name of the room in his/her house you are most familiar with and under this write down all the things you remember in that room, and then the next most familiar room and so on. Each article should be described in as much detail as possible. Then, at the next oppotunity, when visiting, take the list with you and see how you have fared. Do not be too disappointed (you can, of course, do this to all your friends).

2. FAULT FINDING
Take an object, hold it for ten seconds and try to find faults, as you improve cut down the time you hold it for. The more detailed the object, the longer you require.

3. MEMORY
Take a painting, study it for thirty seconds, then try to describe it. Or take a pencil and a sheet of paper and try to draw it. As you improve, cut down the time of observation. Try this also with patterns, but cut the time to ten seconds, unless it is complicated.

4. COLOURS
It is very good to test your ability to distinguish colours. You might think it is simple, but it is very important. For example,

you might suddenly discover that you are colour blind, or failing that, not able to distinguish certain colours. The test is to get two British Standard Colour Cards, which are available in paint stores, one with names and one without (just colour numbers). Now test yourself by naming the unnamed card, and compare it with the named card. Another good test is to check with a friend, his or her idea of reds: red being the most difficult to separate, for example: plum red, mauve-red, cherry red, brown-red, brick red, wine red, dark red, blue-red and so on.

Finally, be alert to your surroundings at all times, test yourself over and over again, visit museums, look at rugs and carpets. Absorb their beauty, and the love which went into each piece —re-discover what has been denied to the lazy.

I was asked by a friend who has tried some observation tests, 'When will I know when I am really observant?' My answer was, 'When you go to the cinema, you're watching a good film and you start to notice (observe) the carpets and furnishings and you can tell their origin without spoiling the film'. This should give you a new found strength—a hidden power.

BIBLIOGRAPHY

Kuehnel, E.	Cairene Carpets and Others. (Washington Textile Museum)
Kuehnel, E.	Catalogue of Spanish Rugs, twelfth to nineteenth century. (Washington Textile Museum)
Fortids Kunst: Norges Bygder, Series II	Series II. (Oslo Kunstindustrimuseet)
Heinz, D.	Linzer Teppiche. (Linz Kulturamt)
Petrescu, Paul	Romanian Rugs.
Kendrich & Tattersall	Handwoven Carpets, Oriental and European.
Tattersall, C. E. C.	A History of British Carpets.
Irwin, John	The Girdler Carpet.
Bidder, Hans	Carpets from Eastern Turkestan.
Hartley, Clark	Bokhara, Turkoman and Afghan Rugs.

Index

172

APPENDIX

WARPS [ENDS]

PERSIAN

PERSIAN

TURKISH

SPANISH

AFGHAN GULS

APPENDIX

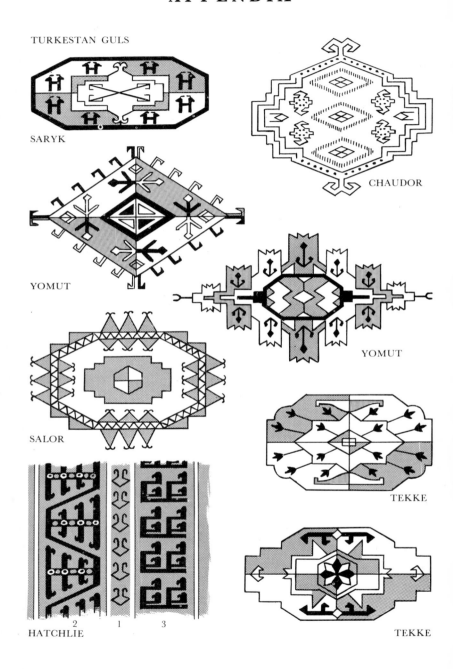

TURKESTAN GULS

SARYK

CHAUDOR

YOMUT

YOMUT

SALOR

TEKKE

HATCHLIE

2 1 3

TEKKE

174

APPENDIX

SIDE CORDS

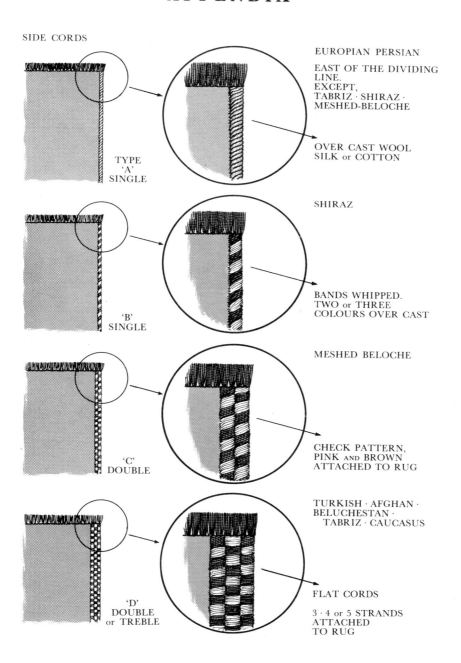

EUROPIAN PERSIAN

EAST OF THE DIVIDING
LINE.
EXCEPT,
TABRIZ · SHIRAZ ·
MESHED-BELOCHE

OVER CAST WOOL
SILK or COTTON

TYPE
'A'
SINGLE

SHIRAZ

BANDS WHIPPED.
TWO or THREE
COLOURS OVER CAST

'B'
SINGLE

MESHED BELOCHE

CHECK PATTERN,
PINK AND BROWN
ATTACHED TO RUG

'C'
DOUBLE

TURKISH · AFGHAN ·
BELUCHESTAN ·
TABRIZ · CAUCASUS

FLAT CORDS

3 · 4 or 5 STRANDS
ATTACHED
TO RUG

'D'
DOUBLE
or TREBLE

175

TURKESTAN ESARI'S